FREE FROM THE DARKNESS

A COLLECTION OF POETRY & ART

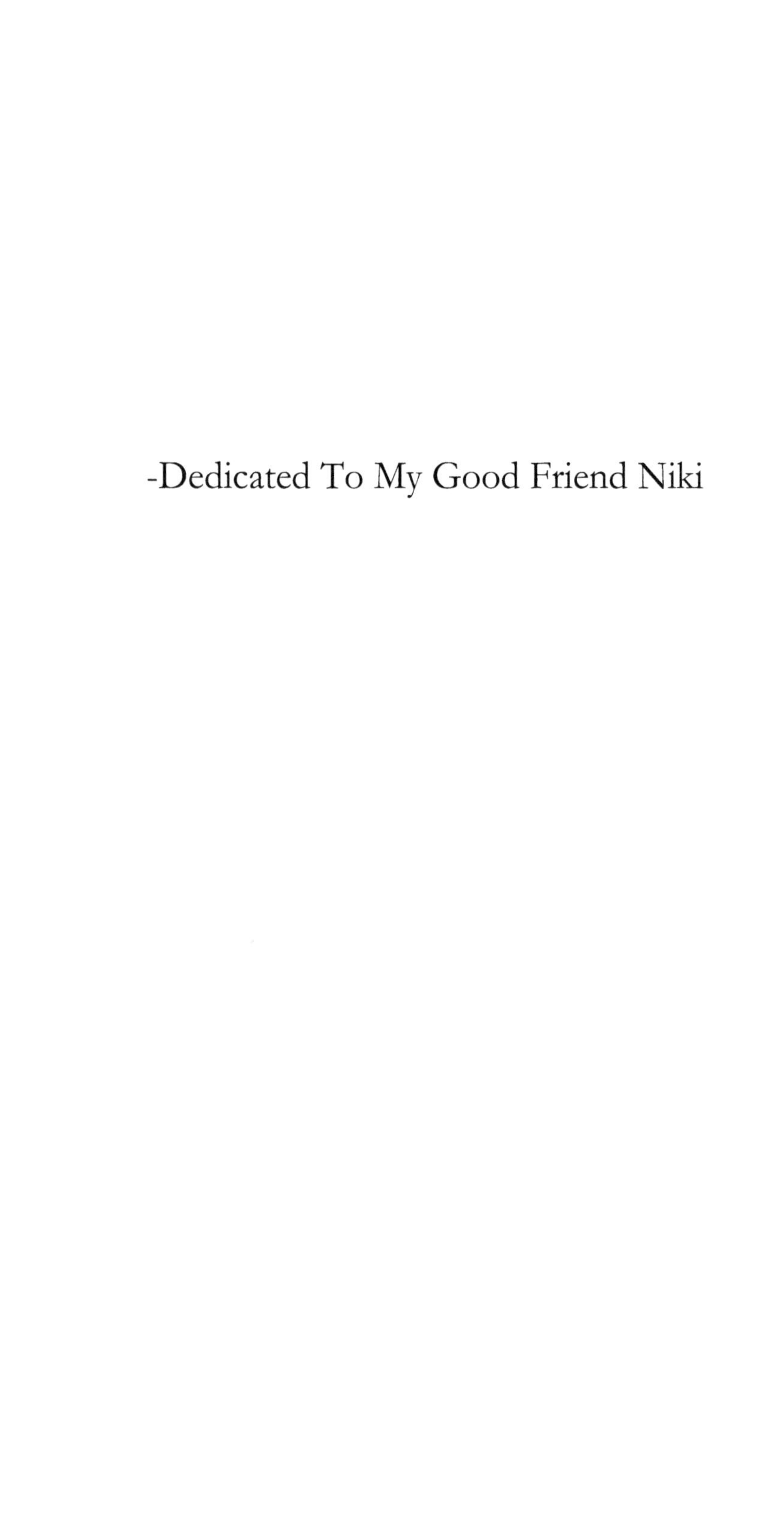

-Dedicated To My Good Friend Niki

INTRODUCTION

I use poetry and art as tools—coping mechanisms—for the parts of life that lie beyond what the eyes can see. Tangible things can be repaired by hand. Illnesses are treated with medicine. But what about the invisible wounds? What do we reach for when there are no instruments to mend what aches inside? Some itches cannot be scratched with anything man-made.

Therefore, I write poetry and create art to conjure something beyond what the eyes can see—something to hold onto when everything else slips away. Poetry and art are my languages of the soul—the words often left unsaid. They help me speak life into the places within that have long been silent. My imagination offers a new lens through which I see the world. It connects me directly to the spirit of truth that lives within.

I began drawing at eleven years old, using art to cope with life's challenges. I remember longing for the cool sneakers my peers wore—shoes my family could not afford. One evening, riding in the back of my mother's minivan on the way to church, I sketched the sneakers I dreamed of owning. That simple act of creation brought me a profound sense of satisfaction—and sparked a passion that would shape my identity forever.

I began to draw all day long, and soon, it was the only thing I wanted to do. It felt like I had power in my hands. Shortly thereafter, I became known in school as the guy who drew sneakers. For the first time, others saw value in me that I did not know I possessed. I often got into trouble for choosing my craft over schoolwork, but I could not resist finishing my latest drawing.

I went from being bullied, to drawing crowds—students gathering around just to watch me work. My shoes had not changed, but the moment I picked up a pen or pencil, people stopped looking at what was on my feet and started seeing what was in my heart. Art gave me a lane of my own, and for the first time in my life, I became authentic.

During this period of self-discovery through art, I was also quietly nurturing a hidden passion for poetry. I could always hide behind my illustrations—they kept people at arm's length. But I avoided the vulnerability that came with sharing my writing, keeping the poetry to myself.

It was not until I began to combine the two—art and poetry—that I saw the match made in heaven I had been too afraid to embrace. The more of myself I exposed through my gifts, the more I was able to navigate new territories and discover my potential as an artist.

Now, more than twenty years later, I still create with the same vigor and joy I felt as a child. A gift of creation, entrusted to me by my Creator, to serve His people and fulfill his purposc for my life.

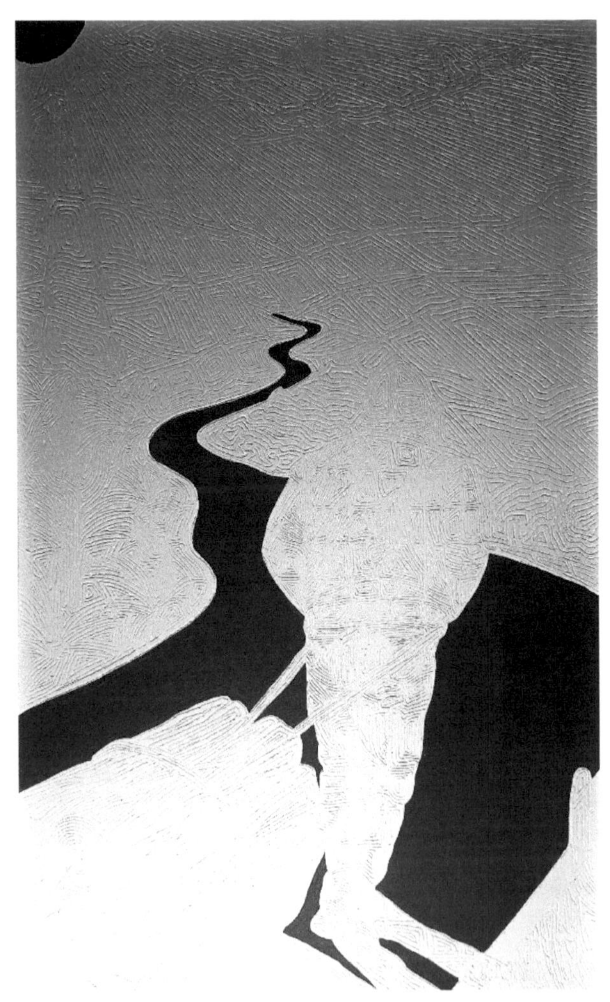

ART- "FREE FROM DARKNESS"

FREE FROM THE DARKNESS

It does not last forever
The pain and the hurt will not last forever
Eventually, the chaos will come to an end
There will be a day when the sun will shine,
And you will feel the warmth of its rays on your skin
The wind will blow in the midst of the silence
The waves will calm and the seas will be still.
I remember when the darkness came A knockin,
The aggressive knocks on my door
In the wee hours of the night.
I remember waking up in a panic just to see,
Who the hell it was knocking on my door.
I looked through the peephole to see,
But I did not see anybody there.
Naive and stupid, I went back to bed, confused.
Then the knocks came again,
Only this time they were louder.
"Open the door!" A voice said,
"Please open the door!"
Awakened for the second time,
I grabbed a weapon to go check once more.
When I looked through the peephole
Still, there was nobody there.
Deep down I did not want to see the red flags
Because it would have only confirmed my fears.
My life was in danger, and I was not prepared.
In my false sense of pride and arrogance,
I pointed my weapon and opened the door

Looking around to see who it was at my door
Still, there was nobody there.
Little did I know, it was already too late.
The moment I decided to open that door,
Was the moment I let the darkness in my home.
Though I could not see it with my bare eyes
It did not waste time spreading.
I mean it was as if one day everything was okay,
And the next day, everything fell apart
It's like that sometimes you know,
Sometimes things just fall apart.
My world was upside down
Chaos rummaging inside on a mission,
To seek and destroy everything in its path
As I sat in the corner of the bedroom afraid
In a fetal position bracing for cover
Hoping the chaos would quench its thirst,
Hoping the darkness would soon leave.
That was when I heard another knock on my door,
But I could not move because of my fears
I had developed paralysis by analysis just sitting there,
Trying to figure out a way to run away.
But the voice inside my head said to me,
"Get up and fight, nobody is coming to help you,
Nobody even knows you are in here,
So you Might As well get up and fight"
And so I did, I got up and started fighting.
Afraid, taking one step back and two steps forward
I had nothing left to lose, and no one to fight for me.
Day and night, fighting the battle inside my mind.

Afraid and tired, I had no choice but to endure,
No choice but to keep going,
Until one day the fighting ended.
I was still swinging, kicking and screaming,
"Get the hell out of my house!"
Not realizing the fighting was over,
and the darkness had dissipated,
I opened my eyes and stopped my fighting.
I walked through the rubble to the front door
Opened it, and heard the sounds of birds singing
The sun shone brightly in the brisk morning air,
And the chaos ended abruptly.
Therefore, I confidently say to you, keep on fighting,
The pain and the hurt will not last,
It will not last forever, and eventually it will subside.
I woke up this morning peaceful.
The chaos found its order.
This morning, I woke up free.
Free from the chaos in my mind.
Free from the hurt and the pain it caused.
This morning, I woke up Free from the darkness.

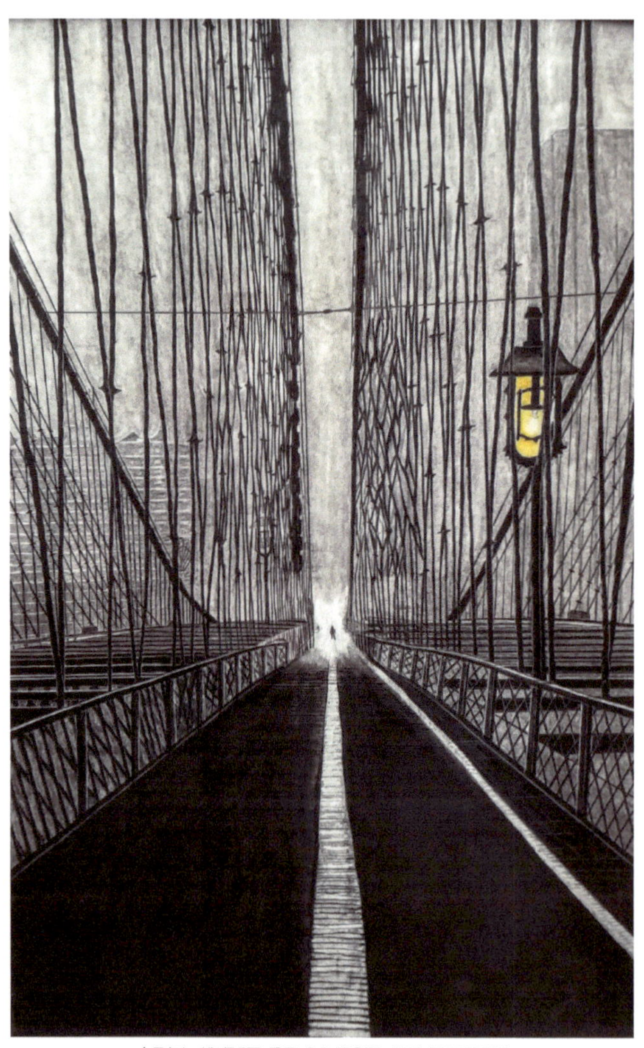

ART- "THE PROMISE OF HOPE"

PROMISE OF HOPE

Can you believe I almost gave up,
I almost gave up on my dreams.
I almost walked away,
Not knowing just how close I came.
You see my dream, is also my burden.
Though it carries a promise,
A promise of hope,
A promise of things to come,
But of things not yet seen,
It also weighs me down, and takes a toll on me.
I have put my all into what I believe,
Put it all on the line and sacrificed for my dreams.
Year after year, I have labored to not much avail,
Critically implementing different combinations,
Anxiously waiting to exhale.
Just to fall back down.
Oh the frustration of knowing who you are,
And knowing who you have the capacity to be,
Yet, being stuck in a system of daily servitude,
Bound by the safety net
That generates your bottom line.
What an oxymoron it is to have stability,
While life wreaks havoc on your mind.
The enigma of being physically free,
Yet mentally enslaved.
I prayed to be an anomaly
As I searched for a better way.

But one day, I just started walking,
I walked through the darkness until I saw the light.

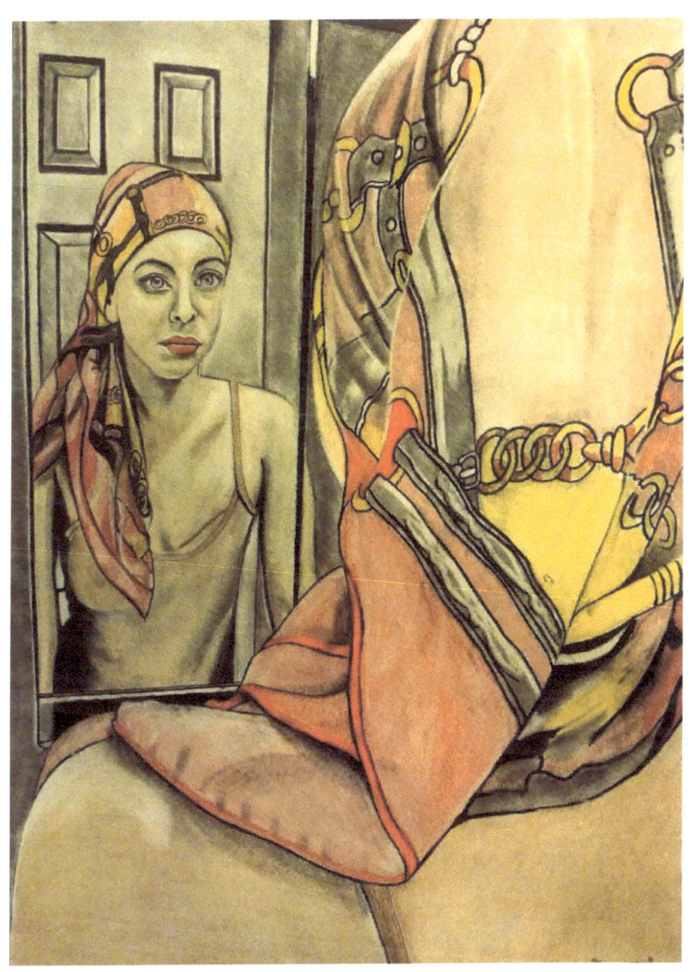

ART- “BELLE FEMME”

WHO ARE WE

I see you, you see me,
Tell me—who, who are we.
I see strong, I see weak,
Are we poor, or are we rich.
I see strength to go on,
Is this where, we belong.
I see hope in our eyes,
The element of strength in disguise.
We need change, and we need it now,
If we are to prevail and stay around.
I see new, I see old,
I hear talk, but I am not sold.
I feel fear, and I feel joy,
I sense life—but can it mold?
And become something true,
Not just for me, but for you.
For the world and for our race,
One as human, one with face.
So diverse, and yet the same,
If we are cursed, who is to blame?
That is why I still dream,
To do something before it ends.
Life is hard, but life is good,
Would you live it well, if you could?
That is why I see you,
And I know you see me.
Let us hold each other accountable,
For our decisions as human beings.

Maybe then we could change,
Maybe then we could fix,
All the damage that has been done.
Even still, I see you, and I know that you see me.
Please—can you tell me who, Who are we?

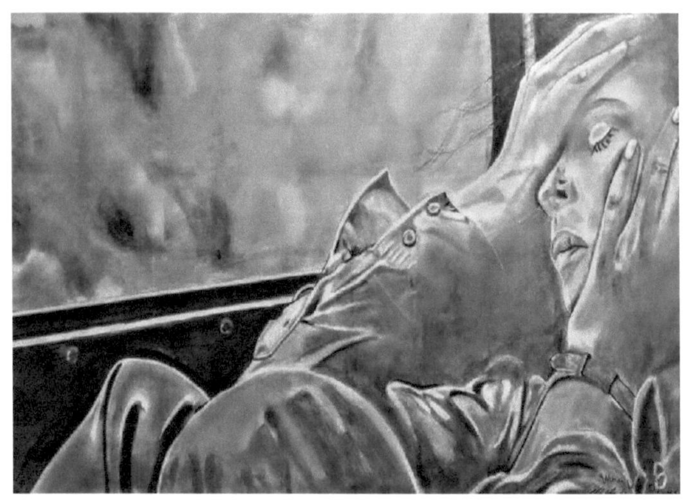

ART- "ALONE ON THIS CHAIR, I WRITE"

ALONE ON THIS CHAIR, I WRITE

It had been a decade since I last stepped into that room. I had packed the boxes myself—sealed them shut and left them to gather dust in the far corner. Back then, I did not think I would ever return. But today, for reasons I cannot explain, I found myself standing at the threshold once more.

The door creaked open, revealing a space untouched by time. Dust blanketed every surface. Spider webs stretched like delicate lace across the corners. The curtains had been left open, letting in a pale, filtered light that made the room feel both haunted and holy.

I walked slowly, as if afraid to disturb the silence. In the center sat the old chair from my childhood, the one my mother used to sit on when she wrote. Its wooden frame had rusted at the joints, and the legs groaned under my weight as I lowered myself into it. I could almost see her there, pen in hand, lost in thought.

Beside me were the boxes. I reached for the first one within arm's reach. It was labeled in faded marker: *Old Photo Albums – Back in the Day*. The box itself was light, but the contents felt heavy. I opened it carefully, as if the memories inside might spill out and drown me.

Photographs of me reflected—versions of myself I had not seen in years. Smiling, unaware, untouched by the weight of time. I flipped through them slowly, wondering who I had become. Wondering what had happened to the boy in those pictures.

Then I found it. A weathered photograph, turned upside down, worn from being handled too often. It was a picture of her—my high school sweetheart. I had not thought about her in years, not really. But seeing that photo brought it all back. The way I used to love her. The way I have not loved anyone since.

I have tried, but something changed after I lost her. I became cautious. Guarded. Afraid to receive anything that could be taken away. I still know how to love, but it has never been the same. I have not let myself feel that way in a long time.

I kept flipping through the albums. In another, I found pictures of my two childhood friends, the ones I swore I would stay close to forever. We were not bound by anything more than our mutual allegiance. We liked being around one another, and that was enough. Back then, that was as solid as any contract.

Nobody tells you what growing up will do to friendship. Maybe they tried, and I just could not understand. Either way, it is already too late by now. All the bad things have already happened to me. The monsters I once imagined living under my bed came to life. They came to life, and they got me.

So, I did what I thought I had to. I boxed up the young man I used to be—the one who wore his heart on his sleeve and gave his love away for free. I put him in that room, with all the other parts of me that no longer fit.

And yet, sitting there in that old chair, I allowed myself to feel again. Just for a moment. I saw life the way I used to. I visited the past, briefly, until reality reminded me I could not stay. My eyes had seen too much. My innocence had long since left.
I closed the album and sat quietly. I was grateful for the visit, even if it was only for a moment. I stood up, left the room, and closed the door behind me—knowing I would return someday.

Today, I live for the moments I know that boy would have been proud of. It is the only way I know to stay connected to him. As I sat there on that chair, the same one my mother used to sit on, I understood her a little more. Alone in that room, I time travelled, visiting the past; Just as she used to.

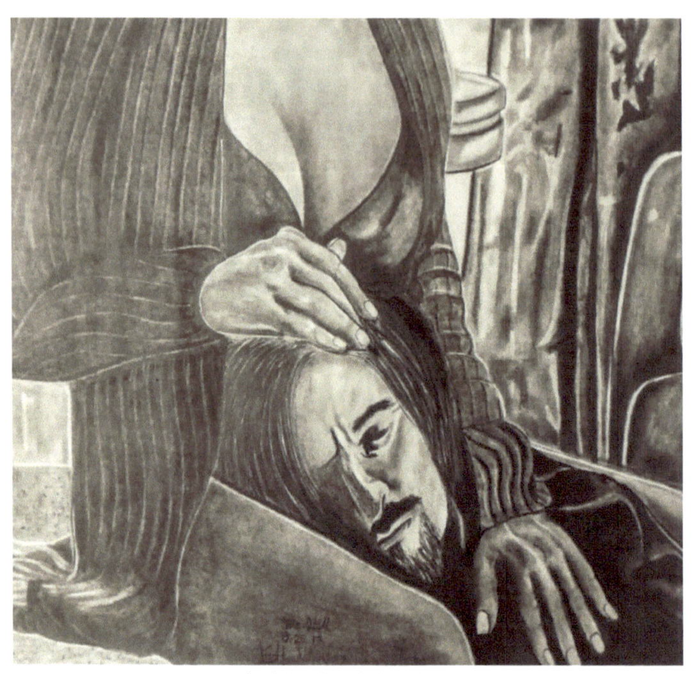

ART- "BE STILL"

THE OBJECT IN MY POCKET

I carry this object in my pocket,
It is with me everywhere I go.
Undetectable, it fits right in, and it never shows.
Although it weighs me down day and night,
Nobody knows.
I wonder, how can something so small,
Have this much impact on my life.
And how can something so intangible,
Cause me this much physical pain.
This object I carry in my pocket is always there,
And always uncomfortable.
The pain is everywhere, and seems insurmountable.
People say to me, just take it out,
Throw it away and you will be fine.
They do not know how much I wish,
That it was that easy.
How I wish I could just set it down, and walk away.
Walk away from the pain,
Walk away from the hurt,
Leave the uncertainty behind.
But I can't, I just can't.
I want to, but I can't.
At least, not on my own.
Sometimes I think to myself,
Does anybody else carry this in their pocket too?
Can anyone else relate to this?
Does anyone have an answer for me,
Some kind of closure that tells me,

I am going to be okay.
Or am I all alone.
How can I solve a problem?
When I do not have the tools to find the answers.
How can I achieve excellence?
When I do not know how to overcome the average.
So here I am,
Left to carry this thing in my pocket,
Because I do not have any of the answers.
Therefore I ask, what must I do?
Where must I go, and who should I know,
So that I too, may be able to find some answers.
Maybe if I went home, and never came back,
Perhaps then I would find some release,
By chance, I would find what I was looking for,
Find the peace of mind I have been searching for.
Find solace in the desert I am in.
Oh what a joy it would be, to one day be free.
Free to experience what it means to be me,
Free to live my life,
Unapologetically, purposefully, gracefully.
I daydream of that wonderful day.
Though I yearn for it, it has yet to come
So, I will keep on walking through this desert,
Because it is not yet time for me to go home.
Even though all I want to do is go home.
I chose to stay and finish this long-distance race.
Though I still carry this object in my pocket,
And it makes my walk uneasy,
I know one day this thing I carry will disappear.

So for now I will keep on waiting,
Waiting for that promised day to come.

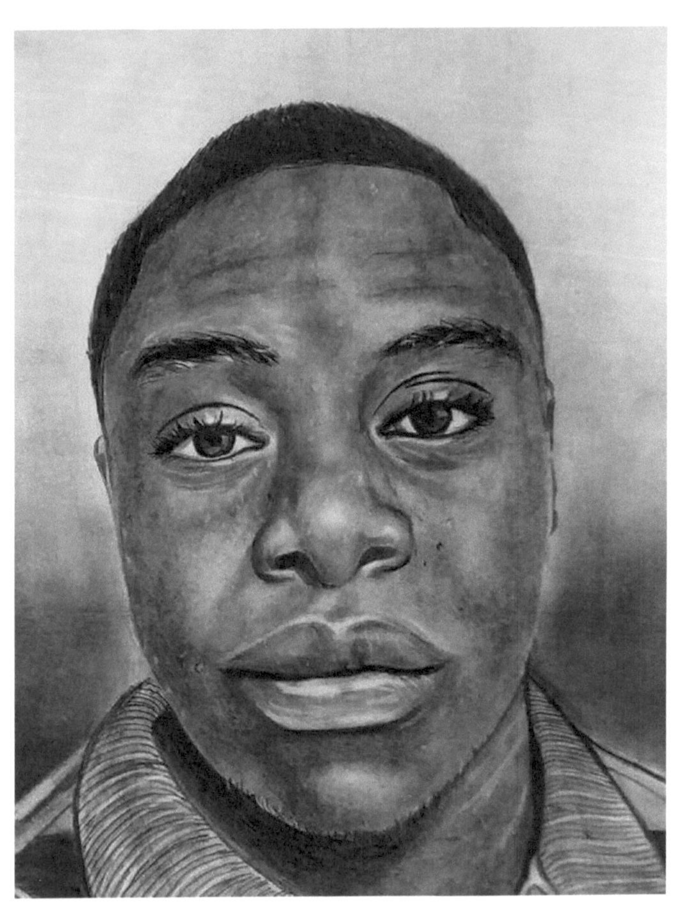

ART- "I AM ME"

I AM ME

I am God's creation,
The fruit of my parents,
I am my mother's son,
The man I have become.
I am my sister's keeper,
And my brother's brother,
I am made in the image of God,
His breath in the living flesh.
I am walking in my full purpose and identity,
Whatever it is, he may have for me.
I am none other, the one and only,
I am me.

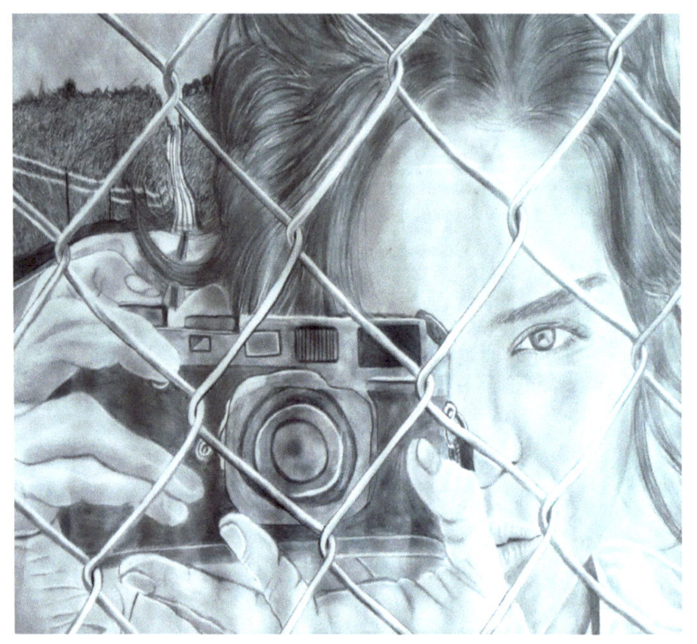

ART- “SAY CHEESE”

ON THE MILL

I live on the mill.
Somewhere down a long dirt road,
Where the coyotes love to sing.
Big green trees that never seem to end,
And in the thickest of it all,
Is where you will find my home.
It is not the most extravagant place to be,
But nonetheless, it is the best place for me.
I live alone in a cabin, surrounded by nature;
Some say, it is the best sitting porch
In all of Loudoun County.
I have the most spectacular, special view.
Every day I see the sun rise,
And I go to sleep with the moon.
On most mornings, I am awakened,
By a stubborn woodpecker I've named Andy.
He is the reason for why some branches,
Have come to meet their untimely demise.
I open all the curtains in my house
And immediately I am overwhelmed
By the influx of sunshine
Illuminating the inside of my home.
Thank you, I pray,
I thank you God for another day.
Another opportunity to make it count,
To make the most of this life I have.
Sometimes it's so easy for me to get lost,
Distracted by the world once I leave my home.

Loud streets, occupied by all the friendly faces,
Bars filled with jovial men and women,
Out to have a good time.
Every weekend all sorts of people,
Celebrating their time off from work.
Do not get me wrong, I love to see it.
But not as much as I relish, the drive I make
When I know I get to go home.
That is when I get to the mill,
Farm animals eating from the ground,
Horses that I sometimes see trotting by,
Groups of white tail deer galivanting without a care,
Birds jumping from one tree to the next,
Squirrels darting across the road
Trying to avoid being hit.
If only they knew,
I would gladly let them cross in peace.
Lovely families out for a walk,
On the pedestrian paths, waving hello.
It brings me great joy to wave back at them too,
Good morning, good evening, how are you.
That is when I know, I am almost home,
A small slice of heaven,
In the now growing town of Leesburg Virginia.
I make my way down the long dirt road,
And as I follow the big green trees
Thousands of them, that lead to my house,
I am grateful to have made it back home safely.
You see, I live on the mill,
Somewhere down a long dirt road.

Somewhere the coyotes love to sing,
Overwhelmed by giant green trees,
That never seem to end.
And in the thickest of it all,
Is where you can find my home.
It is not the most extravagant place to be,
But nonetheless, it is the perfect place for me.

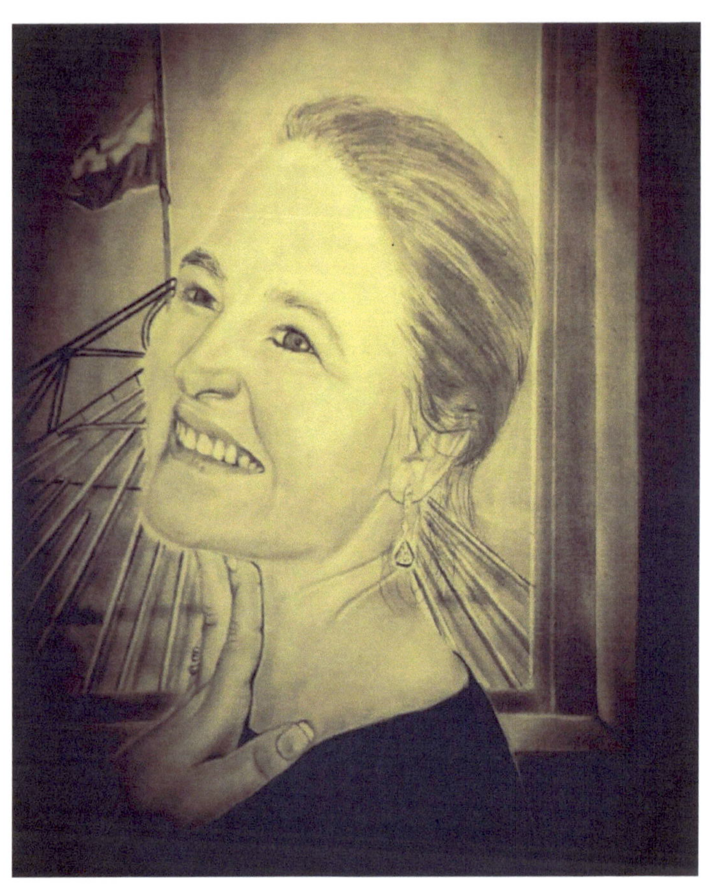

ART- "SMILE AT ME"

SMILE AT ME

Wave, if you ever see me,
And I will wave back at you.
Smile at me when you see me,
And I will smile back at you.
People come and people go,
But our love will remain forever.
So remember me,
As I will remember you,
Back when things were much better.
You used to be my poetry,
The spoken words I clung to,
So even now, although we have to say goodbye
I will never forget about you.
Farewell my friend,
I hope this life treats you well.
And If by chance we ever see each other again,
Just make sure to wave at me,
And I will wave right back at you.
Smile at me when you do,
And I will smile back at you too.
Because people come and people go,
But our love will remain forever.
I hope you remember me,
The way I will remember you,
Back to when things were much better.

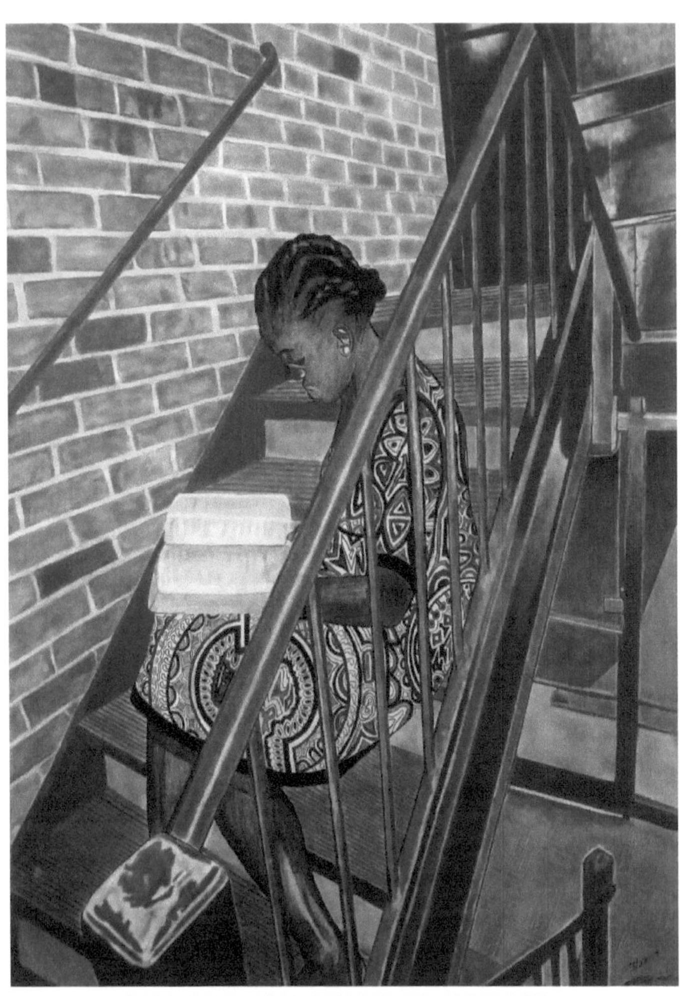

ART- “WOMAN OF THE PROVERBS”

SPIRITUAL WARFARE

In the daylight, and in disguise,
They came for me,
but I said no.
In the silence of my slumber,
They came again,
This time in my dreams, and still,
I said no.
My eyes did not deceive me,
For I recognized them by their stench.
That murky sulfuric smell of death,
The one I used to wallow in,
The one I've long been cleansed of.
I always knew they would come for me.
My father told me to be ready,
Because one day they would come.
In my arrogance,
I asked to partake In the fighting.
The war between kingdoms.
"Be humble, he said,
For the battle is not yours to fight."
He smiled at me and went away,
"Resist when they come for you,
Don't let them overtake you.
That is how you fight,
You fight by focusing on me."
The first time they came, I was not ready.
"Wait! I said, I am not ready to fight."

I needed more time to prepare,
But it was too late,
The fighting had already begun.
So I called out to my father for help,
"Dad! Where are you!
I need you!
I know I asked to fight, but right now, I need you."
My father heard me, and he answered;
"Be still my son, you only need to be still,
And I will fight for you.
Take up your position, and stand firm."
In the midst of the battle,
And in the darkness of war,
I found peace in the safety of my father's hands.
The battle was won, but war will continue.
According to my father,
One day they will come again,
But now I know what to do,
Because my father is always with me.
Fighting battles on my behalf,
Therefore, I am not afraid.

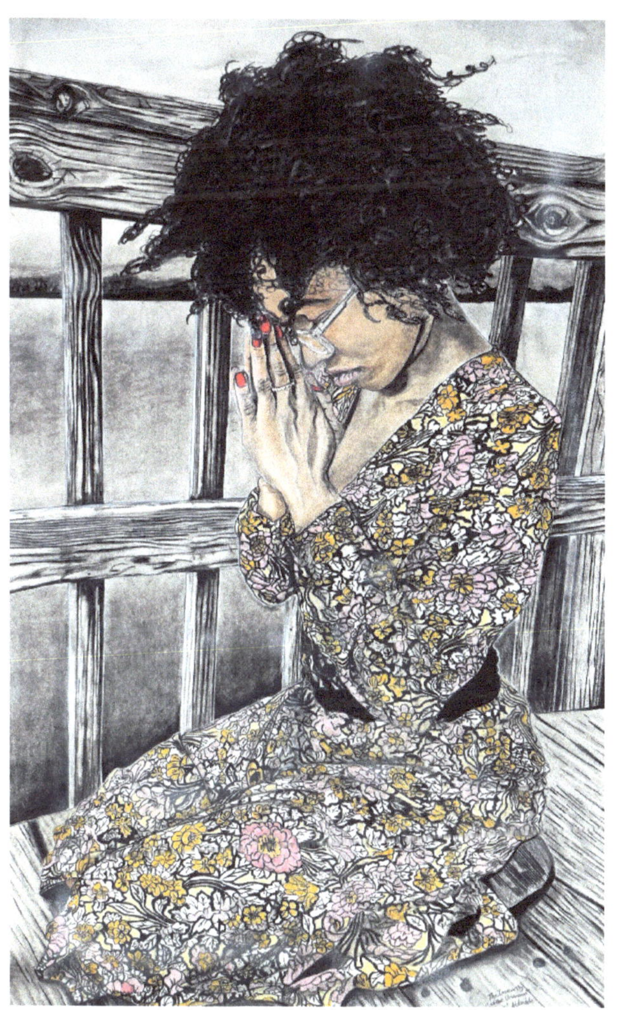

ART- "THE INSECURITY OF THE UNKNOWN"

THE PRICE TO BE FREE

A person asked me the other day,
What I would be willing to do,
To make my hopes and dreams come true.
Would I be willing to pay the cost
Of what it took to be free.
Could I endeavor to endure all alone,
The insecurity of the unknown.
He asked me if I knew,
That the cost meant I had to die,
Would I willingly agree to pay
Or would I cower questioning why.
See, Freedom is an oxymoron,
Because it is never actually free.
But those who walk in true Freedom,
Are the ones who have paid everything.
Therefore, what would you be willing to pay,
For the most coveted Freedoms of them all.
What exactly would you be willing to do,
To make your hopes and dreams come true.
What if the cost meant, you actually had to die,
Is that something you would be willing to do.
Only time will tell, and we all will see,
If indeed you paid the price to be free.

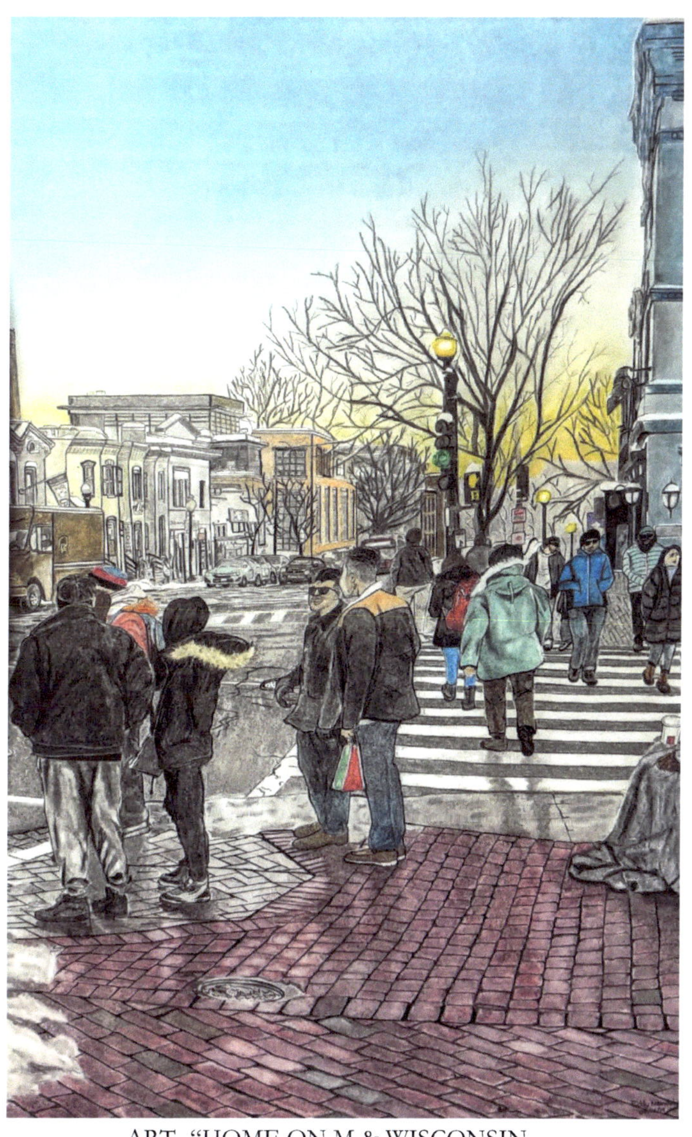

ART- "HOME ON M & WISCONSIN,
I LOVE YOU & I'M SORRY"

HOME ON M & WISCONSIN, I LOVE YOU & I'M SORRY

At what point is it enough?
At what point am I allowed to let my guard down?
At what point am I allowed to say,
Hey, I do not have it all together,
But please don't fault me because
I am doing the best I can.
Or am I a slave to my masculinity.
You see it is easy to say
Men should be vulnerable,
Go ahead and cry, be more sensitive.
But when I opened myself and let the dams break,
Dams that took me years to build,
Brick by brick, cement sealing the perforation,
Reinforced by a thick metal wall;
You judged me.
Condescending me to the place
I have spent my entire life hiding from.
It was not something you had to say.
You did not have to laugh in my face,
For me to feel the shame,
Of being perceived, less than a man.
Rather it was the way you looked at me,
The way your body language rejected me.
You did not have to say a thing,
You did not have to say anything.
For in your lack of speech, when I lost my job.

In the shrug of your shoulders, when I touched you.
In the role of your eyes, when I watched my games.
In the distance you placed between us in our bed.
You see, you did not have to say anything,
For me to know.
So I ran away, covering my face,
So you would not see my shame.
Retreating back to a place I knew,
A place I could escape to be alone.
There, I started building, rebuilding my wall,
Bigger and stronger.
More resistant to vulnerability
And more resistant to your pleas of simplicity.
For your every,
"How come we never talk like we used to."
Every, "can you make it home on time today,
So we can eat together."
And every "this is the third time this week,
You've gotten beers with your friends."
You could not reach me, for I was behind my wall.
My wall of masculinity silenced your voice,
I could not hear you.
Instead, I got a new job, and I worked every day.
Spending my time watching games,
With other men, confined behind their own walls,
Engaged in meaningless conversation.
Hiding from you.
You tell me to come home, just come home you say,
Come home and be with your family.

Take time off and stay home with me.
Insecure by the trust that was broken,
I sank into my seat,
Discombobulated between the two worlds.
I want to come home, I really do,
But I do not know if this wall will ever break.
Even though I built it, I cannot tear it down.
It has become far too strong,
And I fear you may be too late.
But I need you, and you need me,
So I will start climbing, if you start climbing too.
And perhaps, one day soon,
We can meet each other at the top.
That way you can look down on my side,
And see where I've been.
And I can look down on yours,
And remember what it was like to be home.
Hand in hand, we can walk this line together,
And together,
We can build a new place, we both call home.

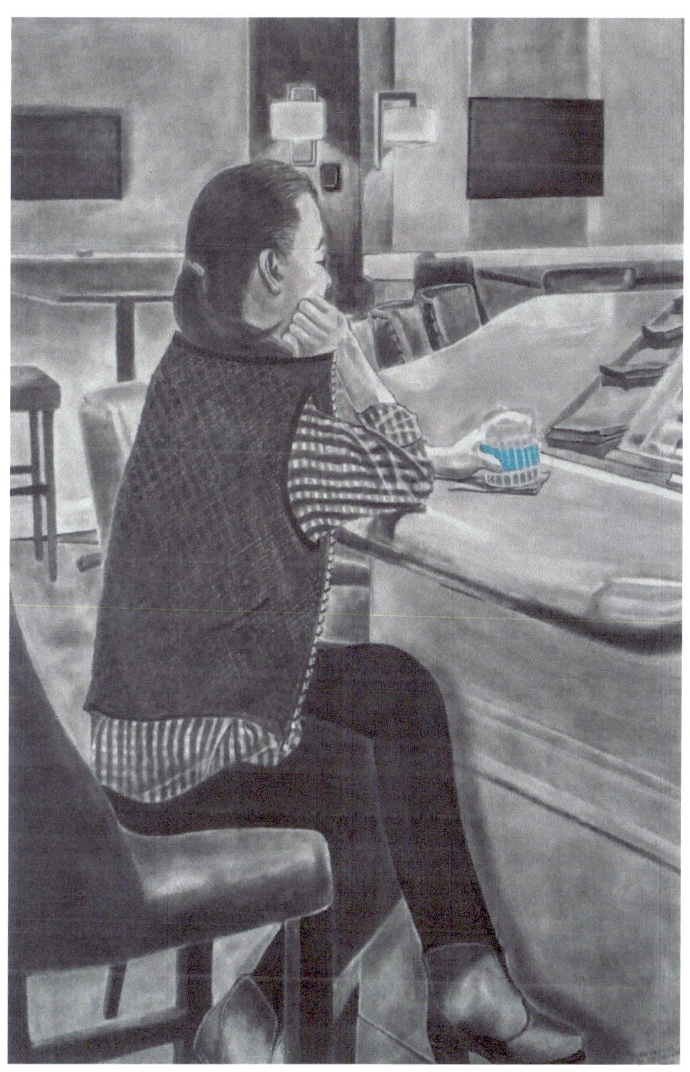

ART- "GLASS HALF FULL AT THE COTON & RYE"

DON'T FORGET TO SMILE

Don't forget to smile because,
Life moves fast.
Do not spend too much time
Looking down, or you will miss it.
Love your friends and family,
Find someone that loves you,
And you love that somebody back.
Do not hold on to grudges,
But learn to forgive and let go.
Work hard in all that you do,
Get an education outside of school.
Be good to other people,
Treat everyone as your equal,
Do not think so highly of yourself
And try not to take yourself too seriously.
Find something bigger than you,
Then dedicate your life to it.
Do not be afraid to feel,
Cry out loud, and laugh even louder.
Be yourself everywhere you go,
Tell the truth and walk in integrity.
Smile as much as you can,
It helps to ease the pain when it comes.
Have some staying power,
Do not be so eager to quit,
Learn to finish what you started,
Try to be a good friend to your friends,

Because good friends are hard to come by.
Take risks while you're young,
You will have time to fix the mistakes you make.
But do not forget that life moves fast,
So do not spend too much time looking down
Or, I guarantee you will miss it.
Love on your family and friends,
Find somebody that wants to love you,
And you Love that somebody too.

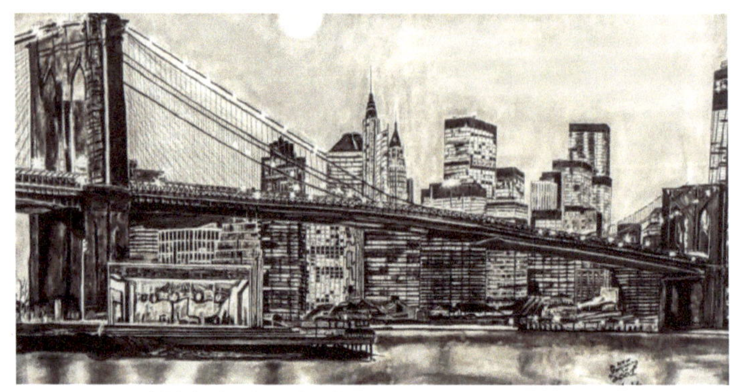

ART- "NEW BEGINNINGS IN 2001"

THE PURSUIT OF HAPPINESS

The declaration of independence,
An idea put in words.
We hold these truths to be self-evident
And try to spread them to the world.
In this country,
Many spend their whole lives being poor,
While others, work themselves silly to be rich.
Wealthy people on Wall Street, in New York,
To crack heads and fiens with an itch.
Some have hope, just like me,
Some have dreams and want to be free.
Some have given up, and some have died,
Others have died trying, and that is pride.
That is why America is strong,
It is the land of the free.
A land where immigrants dream to come,
Because independence is what they see.
Ambition is what will drive you,
So be patient and know you're blessed,
Your faith in God is what will guide you,
In your pursuit of happiness.

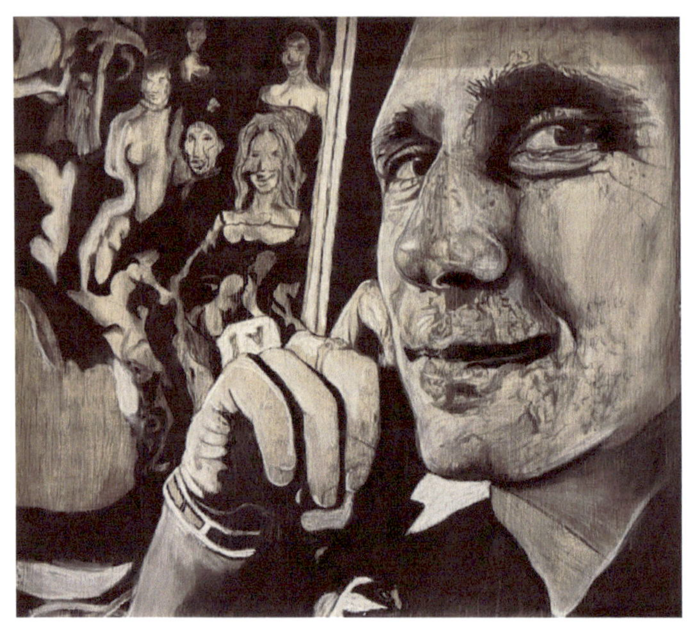

ART- “DAY-DREAMER”

DAY-DREAMER

Sometimes I daydream,
About doing the impossible things.
Other times I daydream,
Just to re-live things from my past.
My dreams give me wings and help me fly,
As I sit in silence and try to make it last.
Some people in this world only dream at night,
Never remembering their dreams in the morning,
Some people in this world only dream at night.
I, want to be a day dreamer.
Turning all of my dreams to reality.
I, want to be a day dreamer,
So that I too can one day be free.

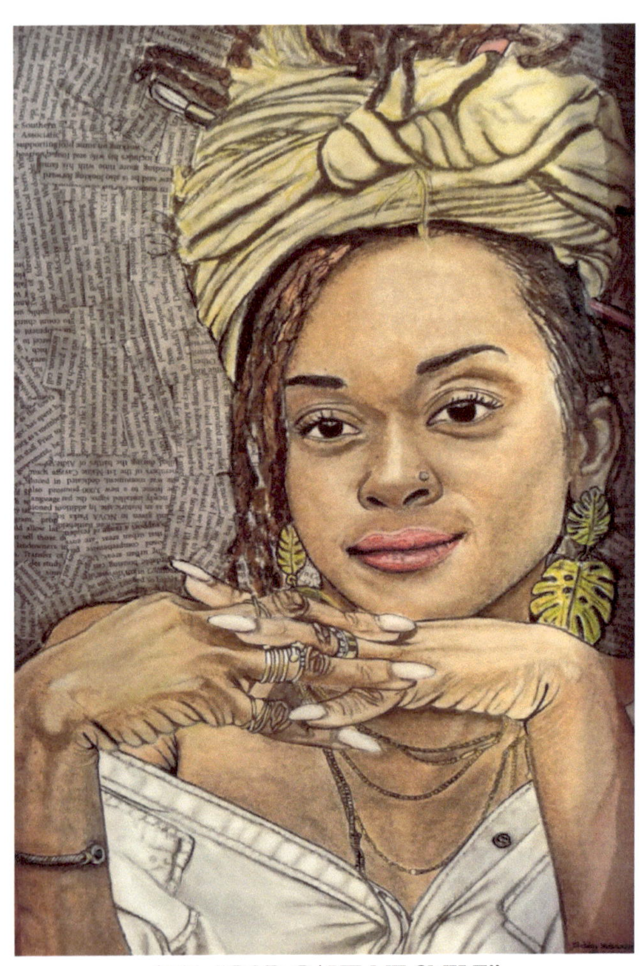

ART- "GOD GAVE ME SMILE"

GOD GAVE ME SMILE

God gave me smile,
So I can show the joy in my heart.
God gave me joy,
So I can know what heaven is like.
I feel joy, even on rainy days,
Because God woke me up.
He gave me the strength to fight away,
The darkness and he fills my cup.
I smile to show, what the future holds.
I smile to shine, what's been given by the Divine.
Therefore, contrary to what you may think,
My smile is not for you.
I smile because I have faith,
That good times are around the corner.
I smile because I have hope,
To be out of the cold, and find some place warmer.
God gave me smile,
And he gave it to me for a reason,
To bring life while I'm alive,
Letting my smile shine brightly in every season.
So, when I smile at you, smile back at me,
Smile all throughout the day,
Because even without teeth, a smile is still a smile;
And nobody can take your smile away.

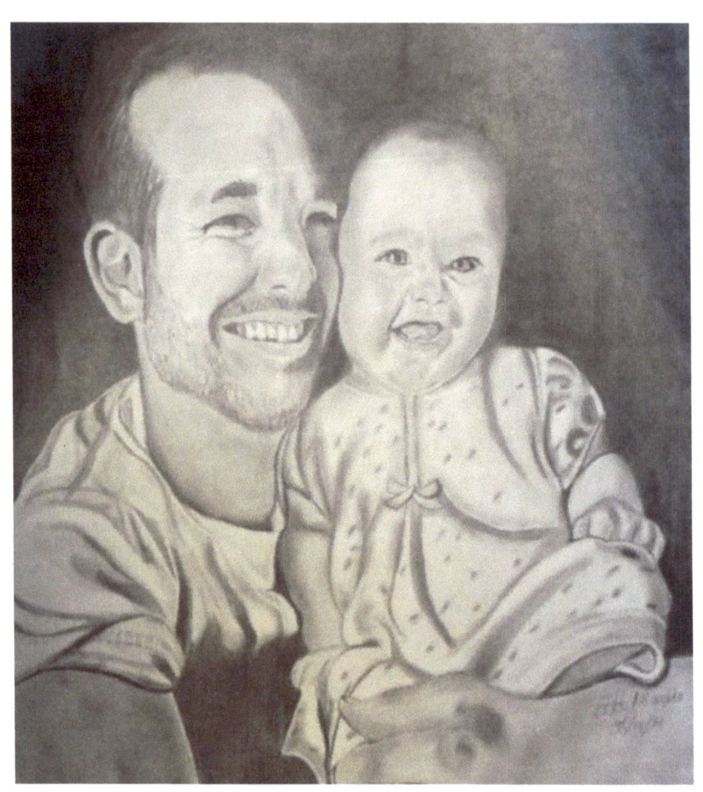

ART- "BEANS & RICE"

BEANS & RICE

I grew up on beans and rice,
Thick, Asian, white jasmine rice
That came in a big 20 pound mesh bag,
Covered with brown pinto beans and sauce.
Although we did not always have much,
Mama always made sure we had enough,
For her famous beans and rice.
Every bite, satisfying to the soul.
My mama knew how to make
Some good ole fashioned, beans and rice.
And even now, although we have enough,
There is nothing in this world like
Mamas old fashioned, beans & rice.
She is not here to make it any more,
But my woman learned to make some for me.
So no matter where we go out to eat,
I know I can always come home to
Some warm, homemade, good old fashioned
Beans and rice.

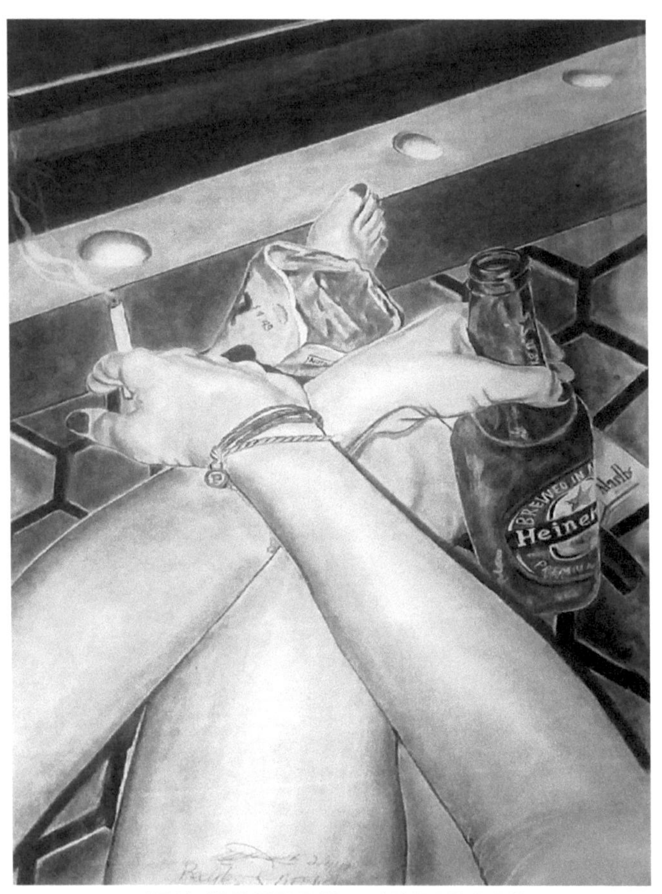

ART- "RECKLESS & AFFLICTED"

INSULATED

I insulate in the darkness.
To keep myself from the emotions.
Numbing my senses into a state of paralysis,
Until I cannot feel anything, anymore.
I do not want to feel anything.
For then I would have to digest,
The gut-wrenching pain, that was caused by you.
I have lost my capacity to endure.
I am afraid I would not measure up to the standard,
Therefore, be overtaken by the incantations,
Taking hold of my mind,
Bringing me to place a-kin to hell,
Stuck in an unending cycle of despair.
I have been there before you know,
And I have seen the burning fires raging.
The flames scorched my fragile skin,
As I desperately sought to find a way out.
So you see, I cannot go back there,
Therefore, I ran away.
Running away from that door,
Making sure to never knock there again.
Because I know full and well,
What is on the other side of that door.
The last time I was able to escape,
But I do not know if I will get lucky twice.
So instead, I insulate myself in the peace of darkness,
Keeping myself from the emotions.

Numbing my senses into a state of paralysis
Until I cannot feel anything, anymore.

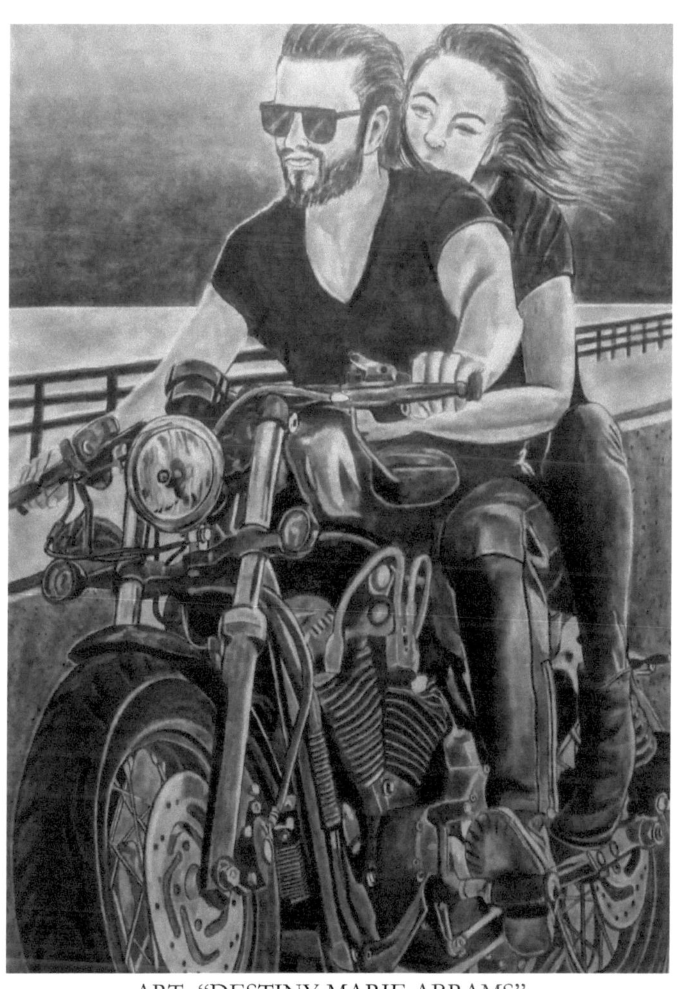

ART- "DESTINY MARIE ABRAMS"

ONE DAY,
WE'LL MAKE IT THROUGH

(Amory Sings)
CHORUS
One day, one day
We're gonna make it one day
One day, one day
We're gonna make it one day
VERSE 1
When the sun goes away
Leaves the night and takes the day
When the rain is falling down
I will be here by your side
CHORUS
One day, one day
We're gonna make it one day
One day, one day
We're gonna make it one day
VERSE 2
Baby girl, please don't cry
One day you will know why
I left you here, and had to go
To give you space, so you can grow
BRIDGE
Because when it's all over, I'll be waiting for you
I'm gonna see your face
And we can be together, forever and ever and ever
I will be right here
CHORUS
Because One day, one day
We're gonna make it one day

One day, one day
We're gonna make it one day

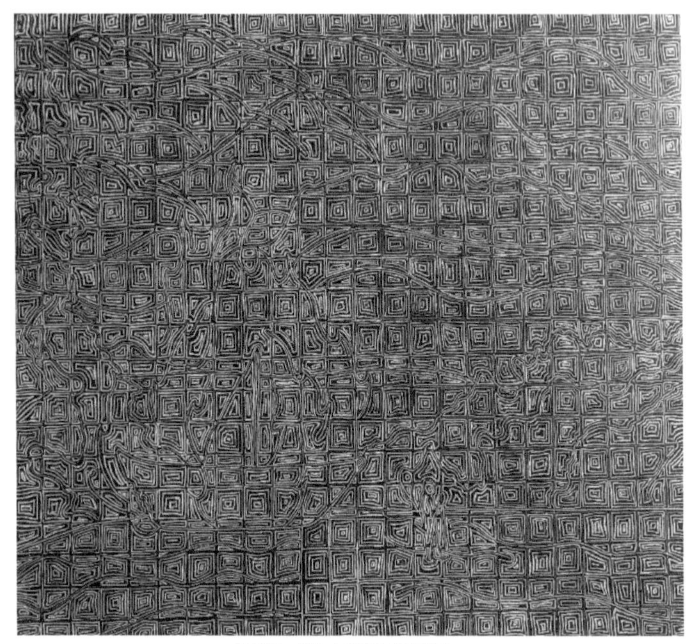

ART- "DARKNESS"

VOID OF LIGHT

I live in the darkness.
The void of all things light.
The opaque and the silence,
That swallows everything in sight.
All of my sympathy and love is made black.
I do not know if I will ever get it back again.
The sun is gone, and I have made a home,
On the darkest side of the moon.
Empty and alone, I wallow in my sorrows.
There is no life here, but there is also, no pain.
Every now and again, I see shooting stars,
They fly by me, but I cannot run fast enough.
Nor can I jump high enough,
To catch one and fly away.
Their light disappears, just as fast as they came.
Why did I volunteer myself into this prison,
This hell hole away from home.
I knew better, but still, I did not listen.
I am the only one to blame.
The only emotion I had left was fear,
But now that fear has also disappeared.
I fear nothing because I feel nothing.
So, I wait patiently in the darkness, looking up,
Hoping to catch a star to take me home.

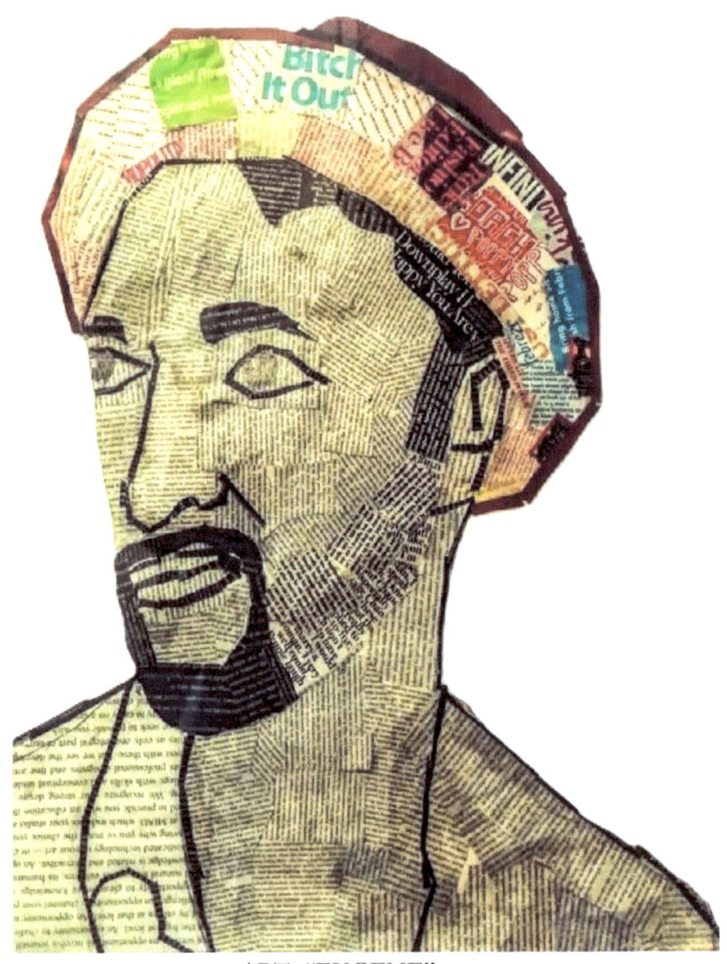

ART- "EUGENE"

HIDING

Sometimes I just hide,
Though, I do not want to be alone.
My solitude makes me feel safe,
From the judgement of this world.
Maybe if people did not see me,
Then they would not get the chance to judge me.
And I would take my time to develop the real me.
And when I came out, they would get to see me.
But how can I grow, if I am always alone?
How will I prevail, if I am afraid to leave my home?
The world is so cold and dirty.
I do not want to give anyone the chance to hurt me.

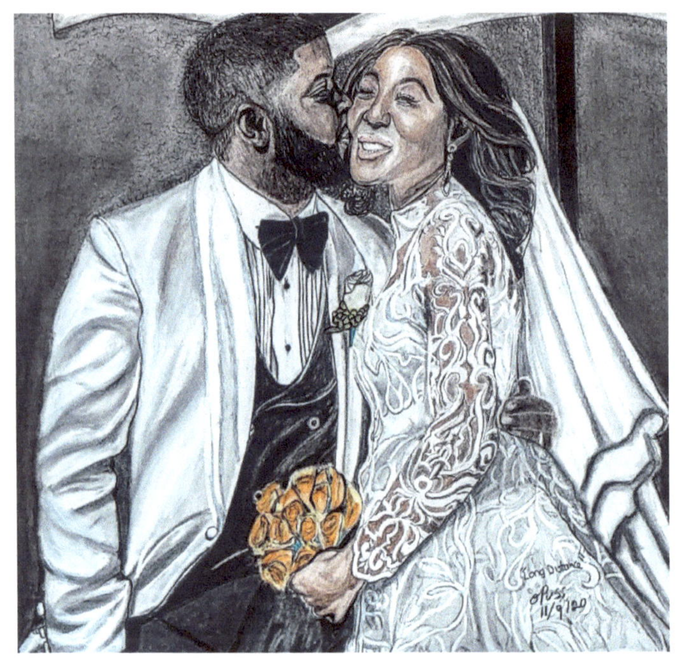

ART- "LONG DISTANCE"

HER LOVE GIVES ME ENERGY

When I think about her
It's a sweet love.
It makes me want to dance.
Makes me want to fight.
Makes me want to smile.
My love for her gives me energy.
I can go on forever, to my own folly,
Knowing my efforts will benefit only her.
She makes my folly worth it.
God himself provides me with the capacity for more,
I never run out of love to give.
She is beautiful to me,
In ways I do not understand.
I like to think about her,
Just to have a better day.
I would suffer for her.
I would laugh and cry for her.
I would give up my peace and quiet for her.
I would die for her.

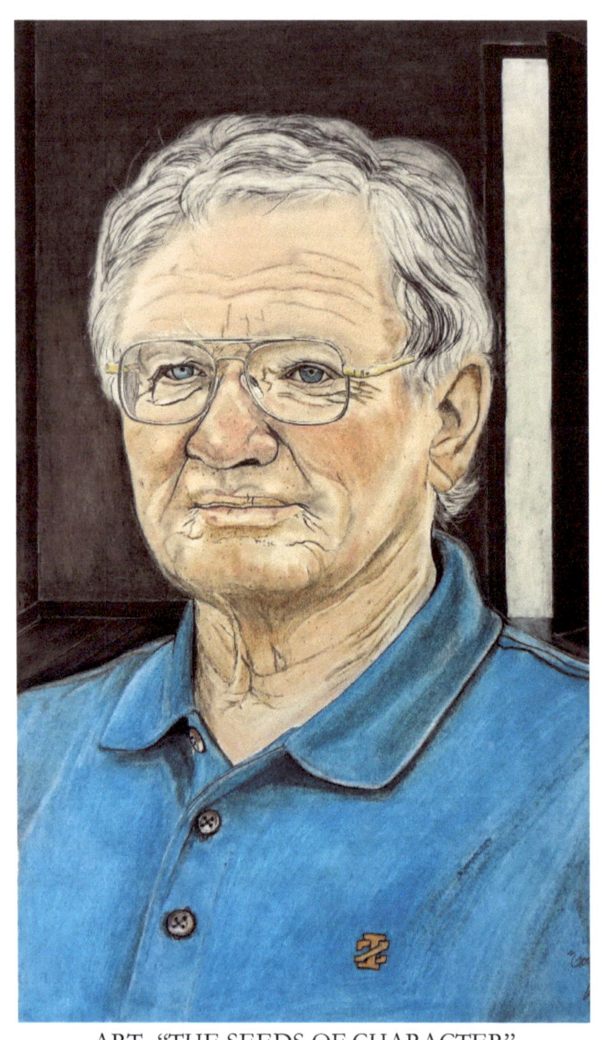

ART- “THE SEEDS OF CHARACTER”

THE SEEDS OF CHARACTER

A steadfast character
Is the proof of an honorable man,
Revenge is the seed for failure,
While love is the seed for life.
Anger is the seed for destruction,
And words are the seeds for relationship.
Patience is the seed for understanding,
As the seed for access is honor.
Therefore, sow your seed well,
And in love and happiness
May that seed help you dwell.

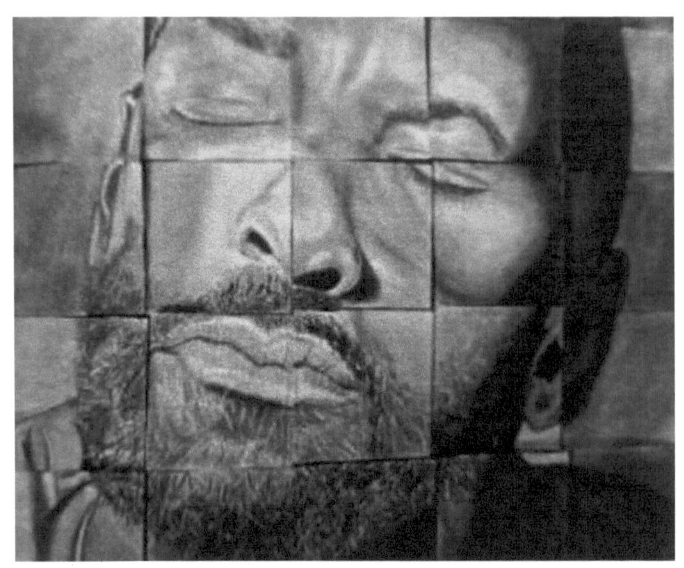

ART- "NOTHING TO SAY"

A WHOLE LOT OF NOTHING

Sometimes I feel like writing
But I do not have anything to say.
I sit and try to conjure up something deep,
But I always just end up falling asleep.
Sometimes, I even have a subject on my mind
And I look for the right words to say,
But I get distracted, and the inspiration goes away.
I mean I tell you,
Sometimes I am on the verge of tears.
I sit in silence, waiting for the right words to come,
Writing in my notepad, until all my words are gone.
Just to look down and see,
Everything I wrote was dumb.
And in all actuality, I really had nothing at all to say.
So I decided today,
To write about absolutely nothing at all.
Perhaps I will have something worthwhile tomorrow,
But for today, just for today,
I really do not have anything to say.

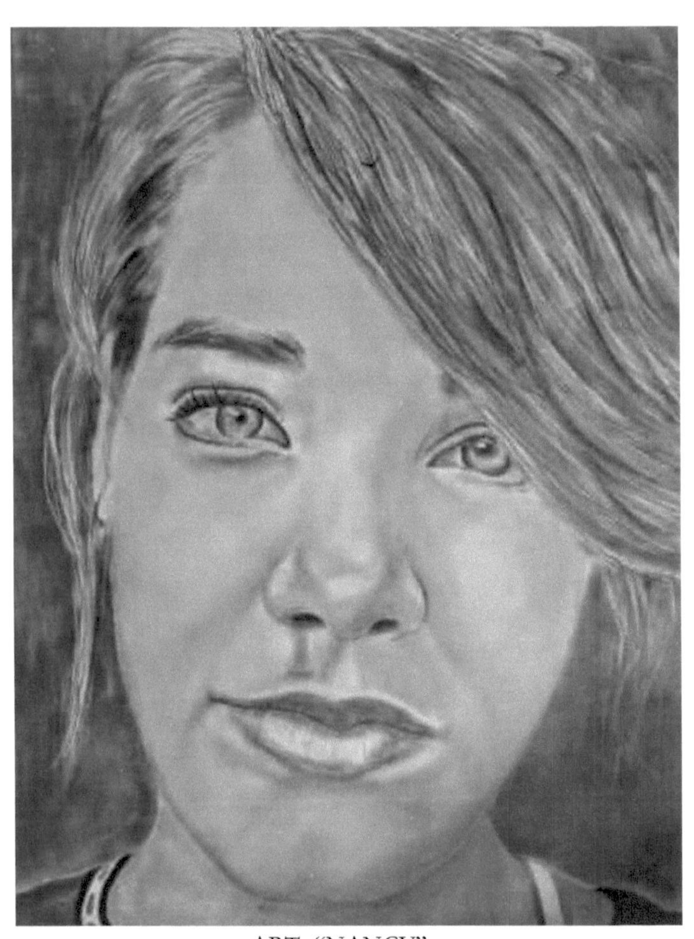

ART- "NANCY"

BUS STOP

It is twenty degrees outside,
At the bus stop, waiting for the bus to arrive.
When will it get here, I don't know,
The schedule always seems to fluctuate.
So, there is nothing I can do but wait.
I contemplate whether to stay in the cold,
Or just go home.
I have frozen tears rolling down my cheeks.
My nose has turned into a leaky faucet.
Dripping ice cold snot,
I do not feel any of it.
It has been a while, and I think to myself,
When will this stupid bus arrive?
Then I hear the roar of the heavy engine,
So I know the bus is near.
The angry lady next to me yells,
"Its about damn time!"
I look up and see the bus making its way to us.
We finally get on the bus,
And it is just as wonderful, as I thought it would be.
Warm smiling faces sitting down,
Everyone oblivious, as to what we had just endured.
I take my seat and smile at the lady next to me.
The one who helped me share the cold.
She smiles back, as if to say,
"We're gonna be okay."

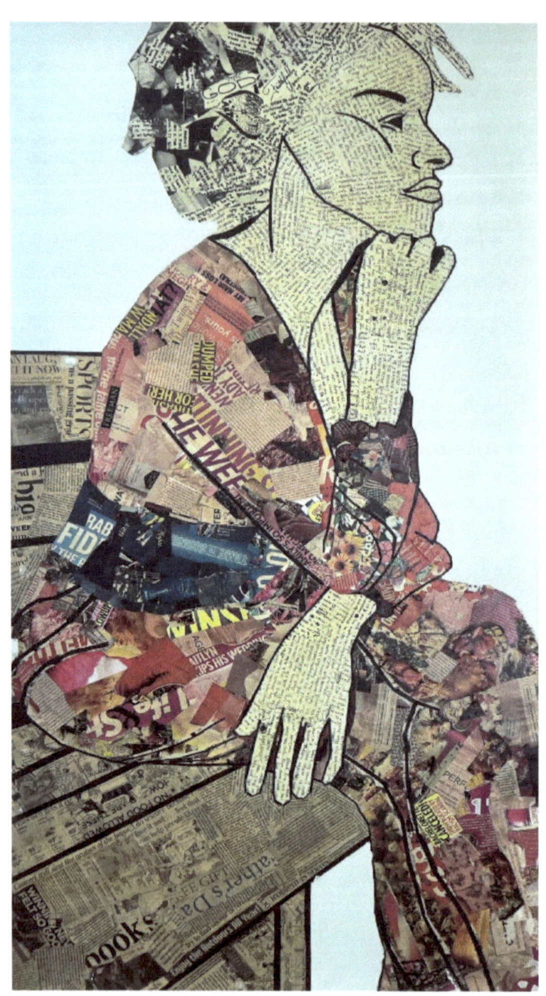

ART- "WOMAN IN MY DREAMS"

WOMAN IN MY DREAMS

There is a woman I write to,
I see her sometimes in my dreams.
She sits there on an old wooden bench,
And listens to the park birds sing.

The sun shines, and the wind blows,
She tucks her pretty pink dress, underneath her thigh.
She writes in a little black handmade book,
As she watches people pass her by.

Who are you, woman in my dreams, I ask.
And have you come to stay.
What do you write about in your little black book,
But she does not say a thing.

So, I write to her instead,
Leaving notes on the bench for her to read,
Hoping one day she would speak to me.
The woman in my dreams.

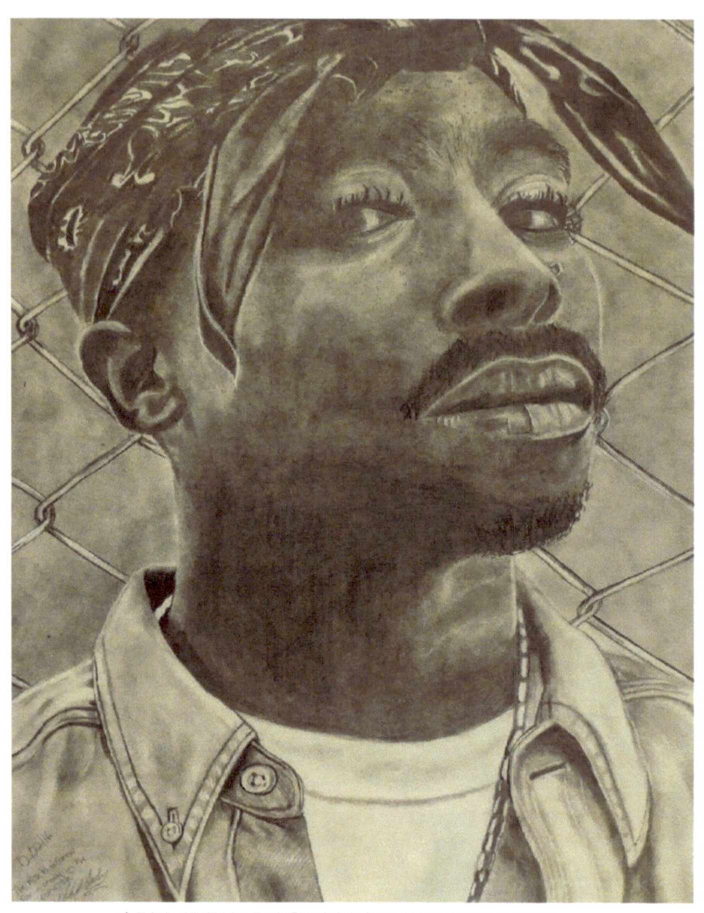

ART- "THE ROSE THAT GREW FROM
A CRACK IN THE CONCRETE"

MISUNDERSTOOD

I don't know love.
Well, I suppose the better way to say it is,
I've never felt love.
I do know pain,
That one, I know very well.
Do not get me wrong, I want love.
I think about it all the time.
But, I know what it costs to love,
And I am not sure that I can pay.

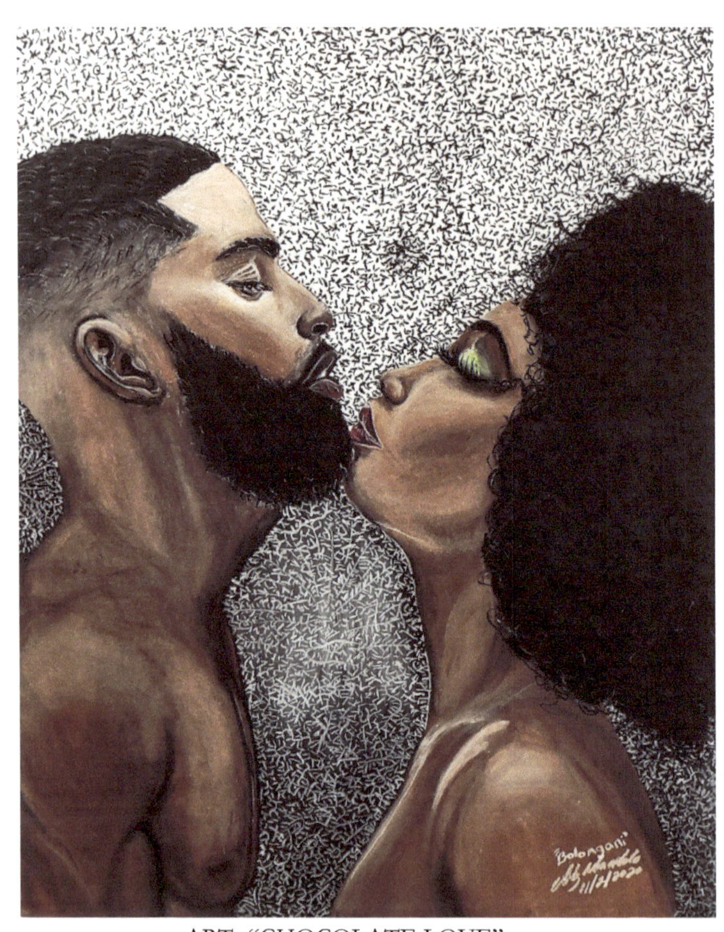

ART- "CHOCOLATE LOVE"

CHOCOLATE LOVE

Well hello there, dark chocolate.
My sweet caramel.
My cookies and cream, Hershey's chocolate bar.
Do you mind?
If I get a moment of your time?
Can you let a brother know?
Can I stay, or should I go?
Go on ahead girl, take your time,
I'll be waiting right here for you.
Whicho fine self,
Over there lookin like, oh my gawd!
Short sexy dark hair,
Chocolate smooth brown eyes,
Sun kissed perfect complexion,
Girl you got me losing my mind.
But that's alright with me,
Just as long as I get a chance,
I'll keep on waiting for my time.
For some of that dark chocolate,
Sweet caramel,
Cookies and cream Hershey's chocolate bar.

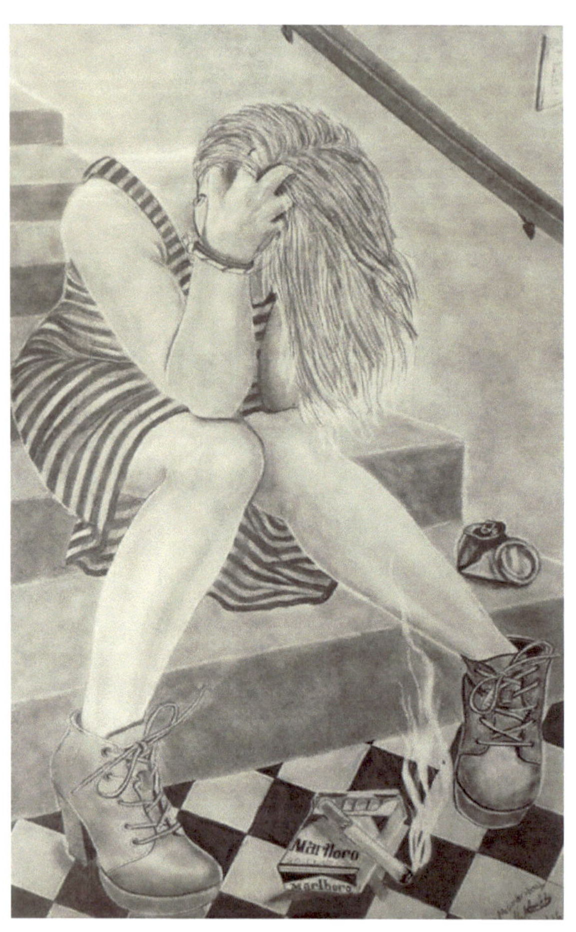

ART- "MISUNDERSTOOD"

FIND YOUR WAY HOME

Count it all joy, count it all joy,
Cancel out the noise, and count it all joy.
Let it all go, let all of it go,
You will free your mind and soul,
If you choose to let it go.
You are not alone, no you are not alone,
Part your eyes and see,
That you are not alone.
Find your way home, find a way home,
If you ever get lost,
Follow your heart and find your way home.

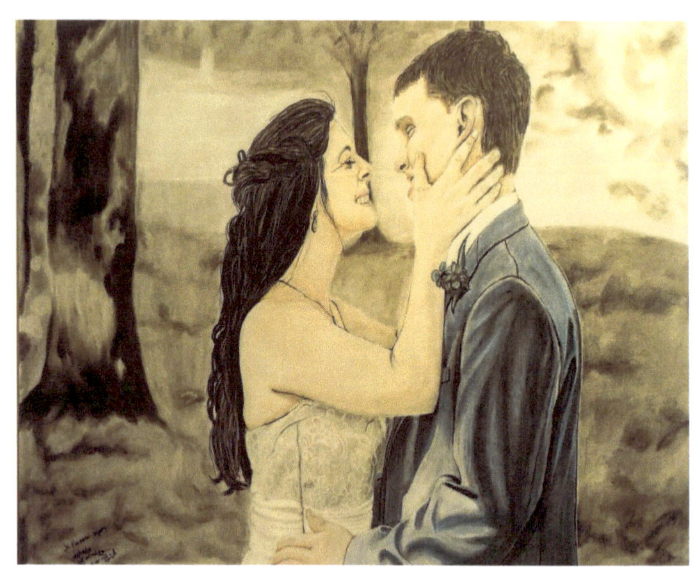

ART- “SWEET TEA & TANGERINES”

SWEET TEA & TANGERINES

I like to come home to a tall glass of
Sweet tea, and a plate of tangerines.
See I work all day, making money for my honey,
Saving up, so I can buy my baby nice things.
Burning up in the hot sun, going about my routine
I like to dream about sweet tea and tangerines.
You see my honey; she's a sweet ole thang,
She loves me like the moon loves the night,
Like the sun loves the day,
She loves me like joy loves a smile,
She is the love of God on full display.
So I wake up early, and work hard every day,
Tired and hungry operating that big machine.
Thinking about my woman waiting for me at home,
I know when I make it back today,
I can count on some, sweet tea & tangerines.

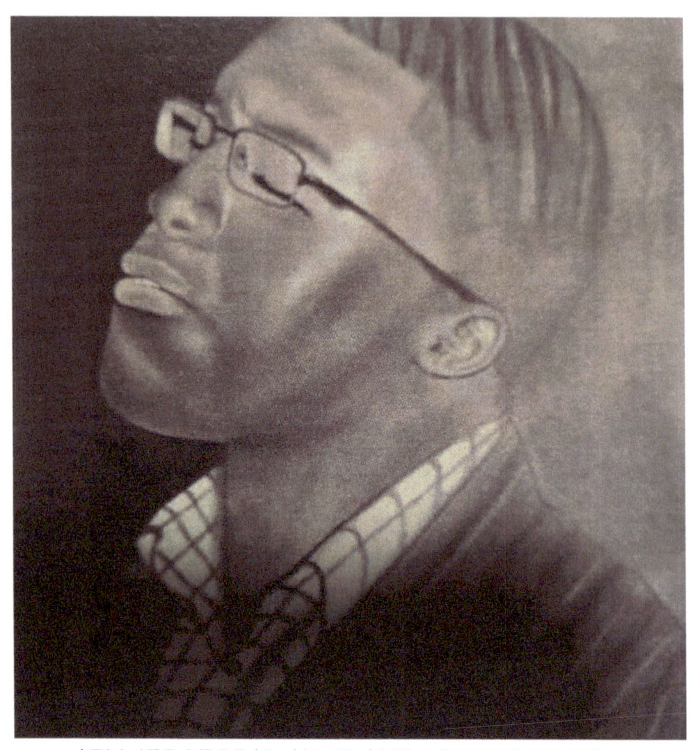

ART- "PRODIGAL AT HEART, I SURRENDER"

PRODIGAL AT HEART, I SURRENDER

Anxious, I found my peace in you.
Void of life, you satiated me with your love.
Troubled, I held onto your garments.
For you are my anchor, my stronghold,
And in you, my weakness was fortified.
Time and time again, I wandered aimlessly,
Prodigal at heart, stubborn by choice.
Patiently, you waited for me,
I was dirty, yet you invited me in.
I shunned you, still you called me your friend,
So, I choose to relinquish my all to you.
Changing my ways to be penitent,
Ye though I can never earn your love,
I will honor you with my life.

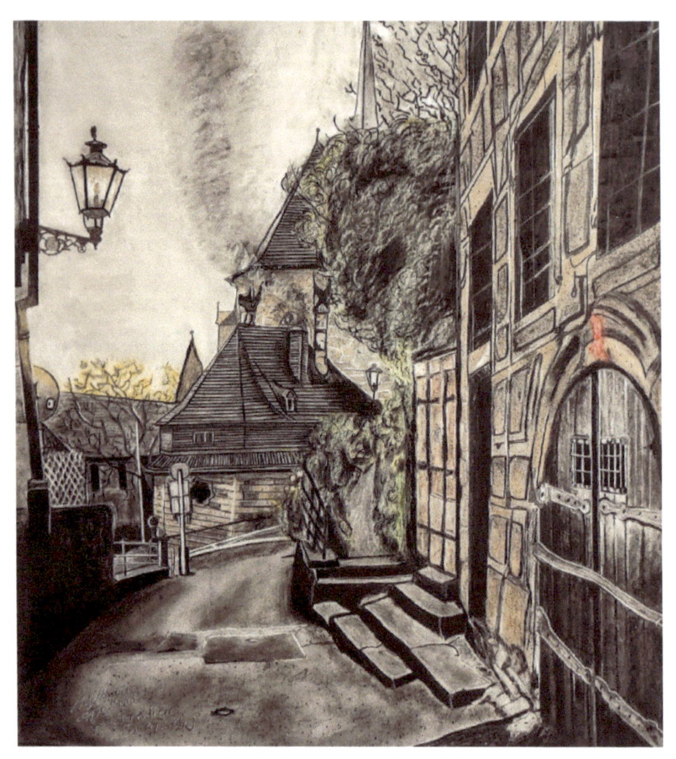

ART- "CHARMING ALLEYS"

I LIVE IN THE MIND

I seem to find refuge within,
A nice quiet place for me to be myself.
A place I come to reflect on life,
A place where God lives, and wisdom is infinite.
I visit this place when I need to be at peace,
It is not a place I can enter as I please.
A place hidden in the calm and quiet,
Found through prayer, and in the silence.
A place where shoes are left at the door,
And clothes must be cleaned.
Hearts, must be opened
Where the darkness is broken.
My mind is a place of wonder,
A land of healing and freedom.
I am spirit,
Therefore, I live in the mind.

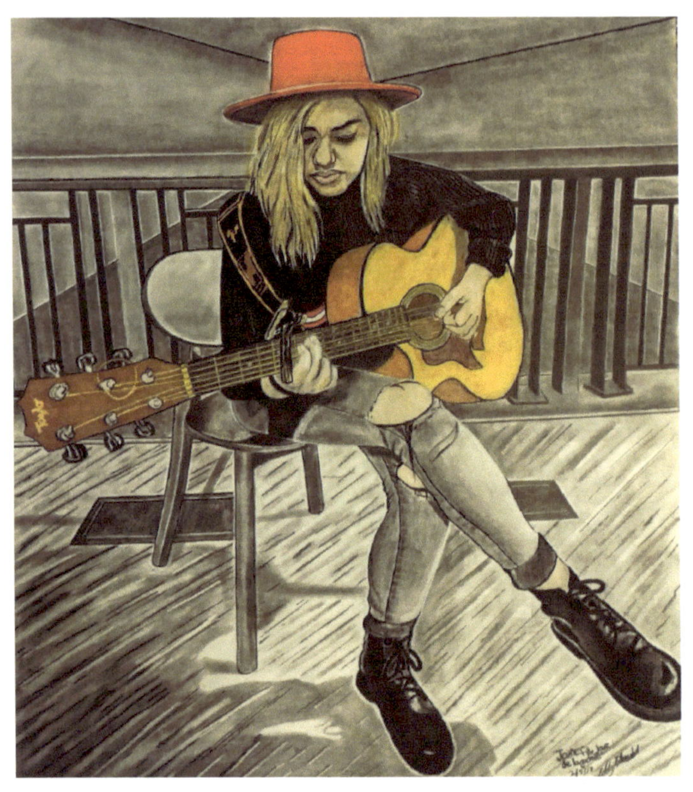

ART- "JEUENE FILLE"

LET THE MUSIC PLAY

Keep quiet and let the music play.
Play music when you do not know how to feel.
When there is no place for you to be,
When things are bad, and when things are good,
Music has a way to express feelings for you.
So let the music play, Let the music play.
Play music out loud, and all throughout the day.
Open your ears and listen to the lyrics,
Lyrics that encourage and bring you peace.
Find your hope and peace through the melody,
Travel through time, with your memories.
So just keep quiet and play some music,
Play the music that lives inside of you.
When too much has been said,
And there is nothing more to say,
Just keep quiet, and let the music play.

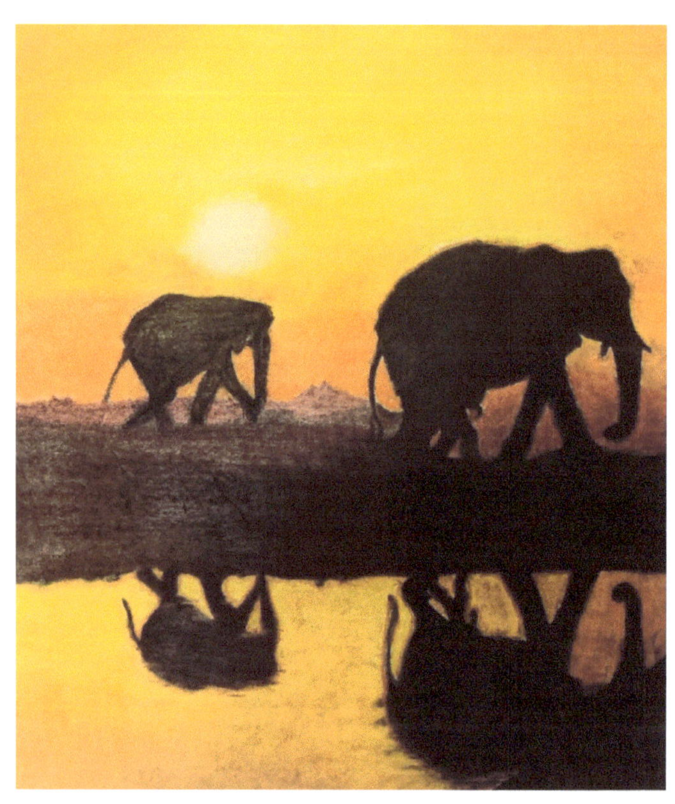

ART- “ELAPHANTS”

LET IT RAIN

Nobody likes the storm
If they have to be outside.
Nobody chooses the open,
When it is time to hide.
When the storm is here,
You cover up to stay dry.
Bringing in the homeless,
Saving them from the storm.
It does not matter who is rich,
Nor does it matter who is not.
The storm does not care whose failing,
Nor does it care who is on top.
So we should all learn from the storms,
The ones that can destroy our homes.
It is because of the storm
That we can appreciate the calm.
When the sun comes it shines,
The heat feels good and dries the rain.
The birds sing, and the sky is blue,
Making for a beautiful sunny day.
But just remember, when it gets too dry,
And the land dies
A land where nothing can grow;
We ask God to send us a storm.

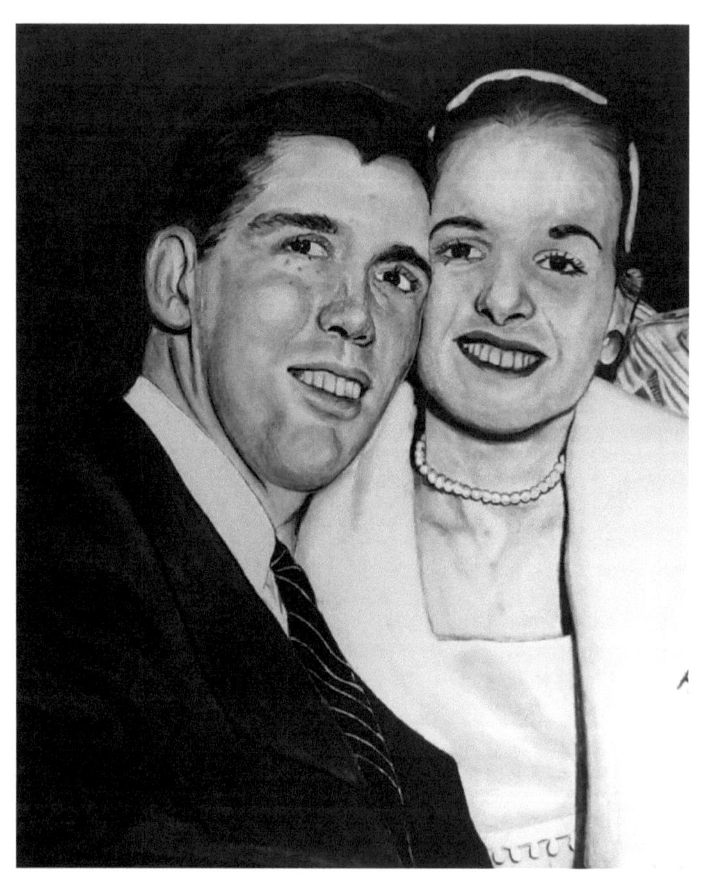

ART- "LOVE FINDS A WAY"

LOVE ALWAYS FINDS A WAY

I have no more to give.
I have given the very last of me, away.
But still, you ask for more.
So I give what I do not have to give,
For, I cannot tell you no.
Because I know that you need me,
And I know that without help,
You would not make it.
So I sacrifice myself, for you.
For the love I have, is more than true.
More real, than even words can say,
And so I give, because you ask.
I have no more to give, and I am running on empty.
But I will always give to you.
Even when I have nothing left to give,
I will my last for you,
Because love always finds a way.

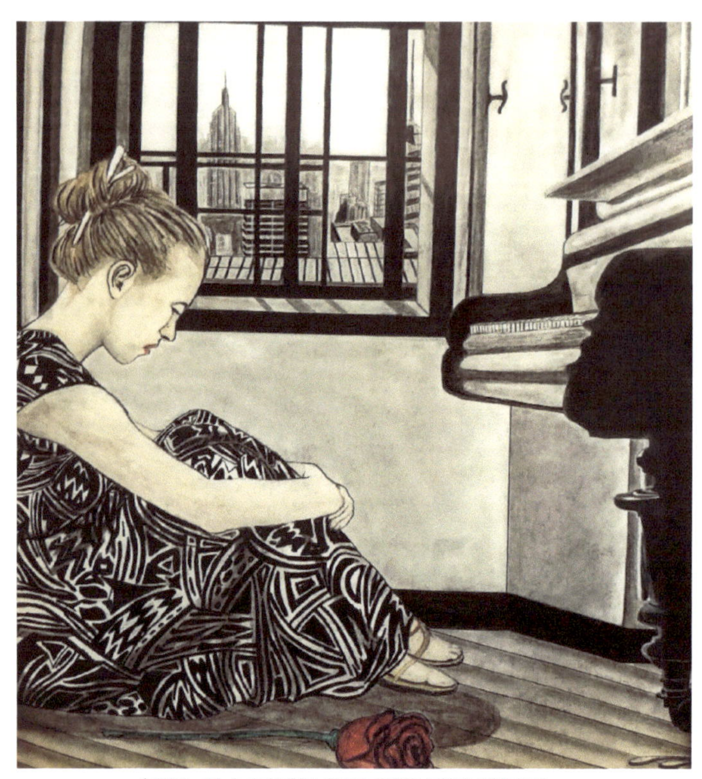

ART- "LA ROSE QUI EST TOMBEE"

THE DIVIDE

We are held together, by a thread.
The very last thread,
On a once perfectly tightrope.
It is the last of who we are that keeps us,
It is the only thing that keeps us together.
The pain is too real, to mask as anything else,
The hurt is written on the walls in our home.
Our family, our love, and our peace is broken,
Somehow, we have managed to stay together.
Somehow, we continue to endure,
But when will this be over?
Will it ever be over, I ask myself,
I do not know.
The insecurity scares me.
The division in our family has prevailed,
My shadow has disappeared into nothing.
I see you in passing,
The silence between us is solid,
I love you and I hate you at the same time.
If only I had the luxury of forgetting,
Perhaps, our situation would be different.
But I am haunted, by the pain you have caused me,
Pain I cannot manage, a pain unrelenting.
So, although I am hurting,
And you are the reason why,
We have built a life together,
And that is a good enough reason for me to stay.

Because we are held together by a thread.
The very last thread,
On a once, perfectly tightrope.
It is the last of who we are that keeps us.
It is the only thing keeping us together.
It is the only bridge saving us, from the divide.

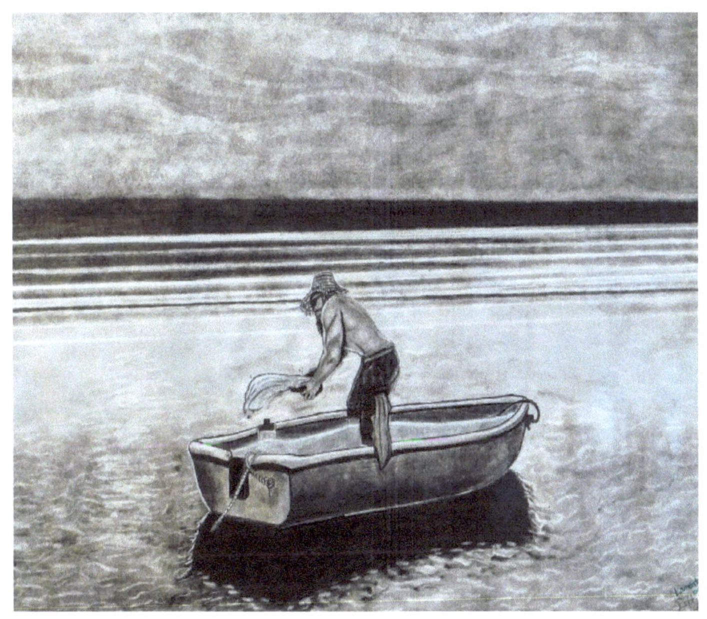

ART- "ON MY BOAT"

ON MY BOAT

I am on my boat.
The only boat I will ever have.
It is not much to look at,
But it is the only boat I know.
I sit here in the open water,
Contemplating where to go,
Looking for other boats
So I will not be alone.
But in my head there is war,
A realm that is other.
Battles being fought
Over my mind body and soul.
I can feel the fighting
Taking place when it is quiet,
The unrest I feel is civil war.
Both sides fighting for my allegiance,
The fight for absolute control.
The war between light and darkness
Must go on until the end.
One would think the decision would be easy,
To choose the light over darkness,
Because in the presence of clarity
All things that hide in the dark are exposed.
Yet most times, I align myself
With hidden things, one cannot say,
Exercised in the darkness,
Camouflaged throughout the day.
Afraid to be seen, I cover my face,

Casting shadows.
Ye thou my heart finds peace in the light,
Darkness seduces me when the sun goes away.
Tormented between wanting to be
Filled with absolute clarity,
Yet indulging in hidden secret places,
And nobody knows.
For every ounce of darkness,
Water fills my boat,
For every secret untold,
The water increases a little more.
My feet are wet, and I am afraid.
Afraid because I cannot swim,
Not these waters, not this sea.
For the waves are far too heavy,
And by myself, these waves will surely crush me.
So you see, I need my boat,
For without it, I am vulnerable.
My father said to me when I was young,
Protect your boat child,
Protect your boat,
For it is the only thing that will protect you.
It will either keep you afloat, or destroy you.
I did not listen to him,
Nor did I understand him.
His words to me were fleeting.
Though now that my father is gone,
His words have found me once more.
Maybe if I had known,
Perhaps if I had cared,

I could have saved myself some despair.
I now find myself hesitant,
Skeptical, as to what I allow on my boat.
Filtering out anything,
That does not produce good fruit.
I have spent years exercising my flesh,
Years more nourishing my body
With foods to help me grow.
I have spent over a decade on this boat,
Educating myself tirelessly.
Yet, allowing my boat to become a landfill,
A place strangers dispose their filth.
Infiltrated through deception,
I became accustomed to the smell.
My stench had become noticeable to others.
I became desensitized to reality,
Disconnected to my humanity.
You see, good fruit cannot grow in a landfill,
As darkness disappears in the midst of light.
One will always overcome the other,
As day comes about from the rise of the sun.
No matter how well you can hide in the dark,
The light will always find you.
No matter how much perfume you apply,
If you are a landfill,
The smell of garbage will always be around you.
For what is ingested, must come out,
And what is hidden, will see light,
Therefore, it is wiser to live in the day.
For the destruction of one's boat,

Comes in the night.
So remove the waters from your boat,
One scoop at a time.
For once your boat is light
You will drift into the path of the sun.
Let the sun dry your boat,
And help your harvest grow.
Take heed and protect your boat,
For the light that battles the darkness,
Has already overcome.

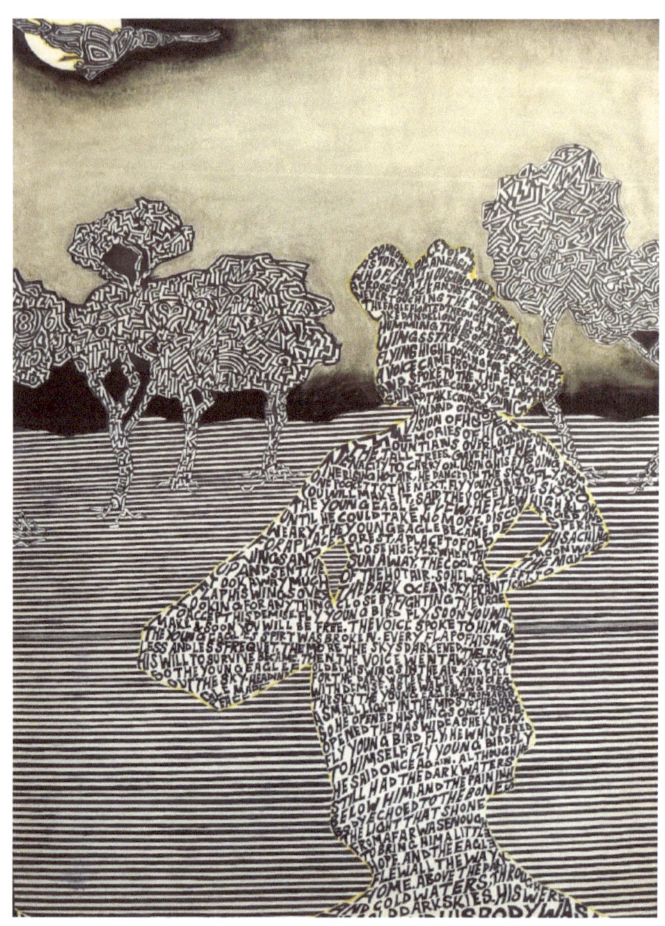

ART- "THE EAGLE IN THE SKY"

THE EAGLE IN THE SKY

Someone once told me
A story about an eagle,
Who flew a thousand miles
Across the ocean just to get home.
Never touching the waters,
The eagle floated through the sky
Like dandelions blowing in the wind.
Humming tunes of freedom to itself.
Wings stretched wide open,
Flying high looking for dry land.
A voice came from the clouds
And spoke to the young lost eagle
Saying, "take courage young bird, take courage."
Holding onto a vision of hope,
Memories of high mountains,
Overlooking the thick forest trees
Gave him the tenacity to carry on.
Using his sharp focused eyes to find,
The rising pockets of hot air,
He danced around in the sky,
Going from one pocket to the next.
Fly young bird, fly,
Soon you are going to make it
Said the voice in the sky.
So the young eagle flew,
He flew high and flew low
Until he could take no more.
Discouraged and weary,

The young eagle became desperate for a place to rest.
A place to fold his aching wings and close his eyes.
When the moon woke up
And sent the sun away,
The cool of the night,
Took away much of the rising hot air.
So he was left to flap his wings,
Over the dark and cold ocean sky.
Frantically looking for anything close by,
Fighting the urge to accept his demise.
Fly young bird, fly,
Soon you will make it,
Soon you will be free.
The voice spoke to him again.
But the young eagles spirit was broken,
Every flap of his wings
Less and less frequent.
The more the skies darkened,
The less his will to survive became,
And the voice went away too.
So the young eagle folded his wings in the air
And fell out of the sky.
Heading for the dark waters,
The young eagle made peace with his demise.
As he was falling from the sky,
The young eagle saw from afar,
A small light in the midst of the darkness.
So he opened his wings once more,
Opened them as wide as he knew,
Fly young bird fly, he whispered to himself.

Fly young bird, he said once again.
Although he still had the dark waters below him,
And The pain in his body echoed to the bone,
The light that shone from afar
Was enough to bring him a little hope.
And the young eagle flew all the way home.
Above the dark and cold waters,
Through the ominous black skies,
His wings were broken,
But his heart was full of life.
The young eagle finally found his resting place,
As he laid there on solid ground.

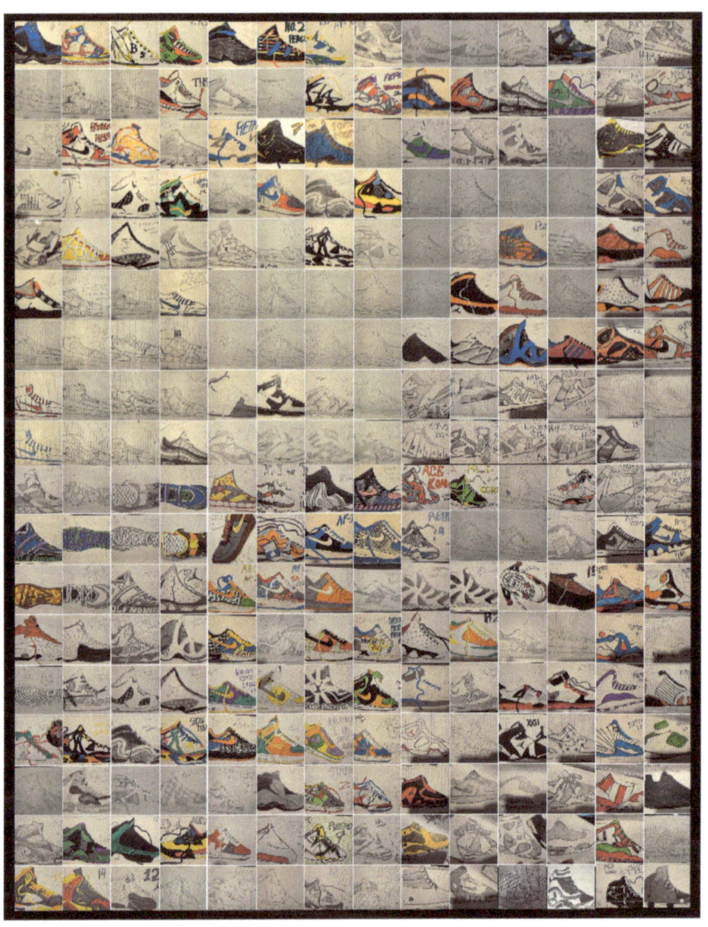

ART- "THE ONLY WAY TO FLY, IS TO BELIEVE"

THE ONLY WAY TO FLY, IS TO BELIEVE

I climbed onto the kitchen counter,
I stood there, Naked and unashamed.
I saw only the possibilities of what could be,
And without fear or hesitation,
I took off running as fast as I could.
Confident, that I would be able to fly,
Knowing my father would catch me in the air.
Blissfully, I landed into his arms,
I smiled at him because,
I saw only the possibilities of what could be,
And I knew, the only way for me to fly,
Was to believe.

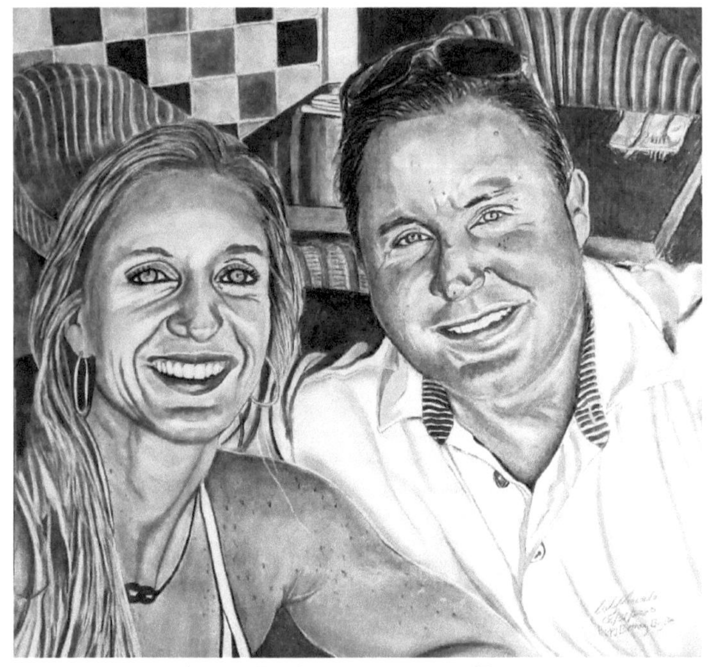

ART- "DESTINY HELPERS"

A special thanks to my brother Greg and his wife Deirdre for sharing some of their lives with me, allowing me to see what was possible when you put your faith in God.

"As iron sharpens iron, so one person sharpens another."
-Proverbs 27:17

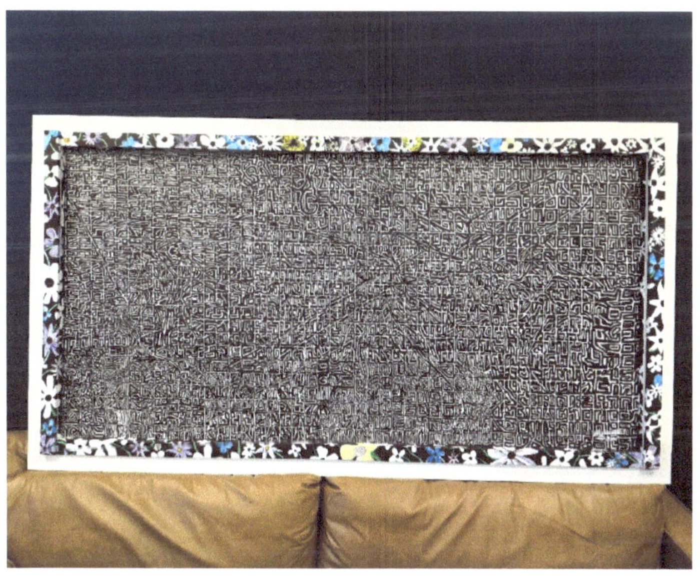

ART- "SACRIFICES"

With deep thanks and gratitude to Pastor Andrew McGraw. You allowed your light to shine on me, helping me see myself through a clearer, more hopeful lens. Your guidance helped me to become more of myself.

"God is not unjust; he will not forget your work and the love you have shown him as you have helped his people and continue to help them." -Hebrews 6:10

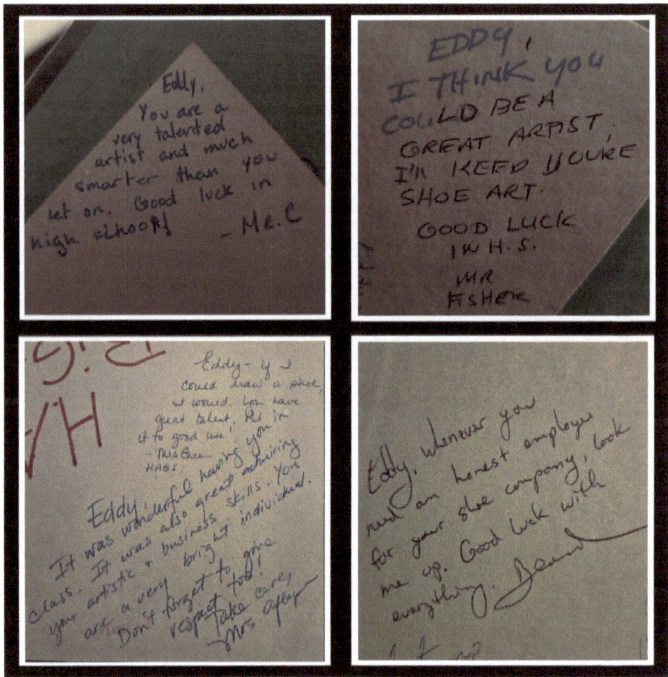

8th Grade Yearbook

An endless gratitude to the educators who saw the value and took time to speak life to me when I needed it the most.

"We have different gifts, according to the grace given to each of us. If your gift is serving, then serve; if it is teaching, then teach. If it is to encourage, then give encouragement; if it is giving, then give generously; if it is to lead, do it diligently"
- Romans 12: 6-8

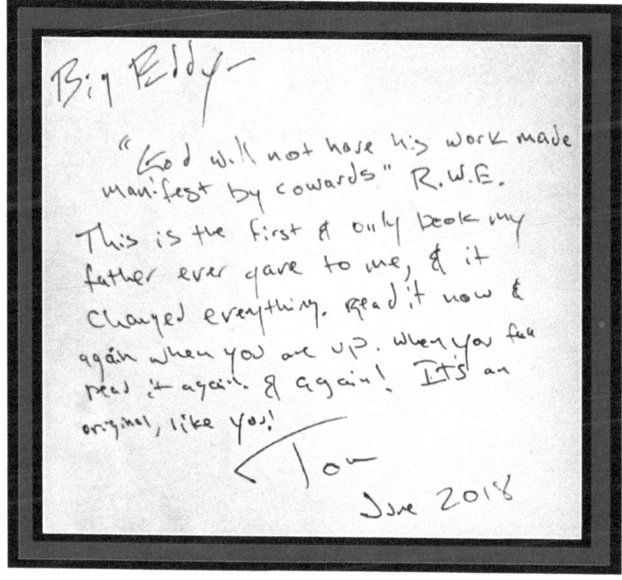

Big Buddy—

"God will not have his work made manifest by cowards" R.W.E.

This is the first & only book my father ever gave to me, & it changed everything. Read it now & again when you are up. When you fall read it again. & again! It's an original, like you!

Tom

June 2018

Last, but certainly not least, a special thanks to my best friend Tom. This life would be empty without you. So, while the wheels are still turning, may the world get to see and experience you the way I do—as one of God's finest creations.

"A man of many companions may come to ruin, but there is a friend who sticks closer than a brother." -Proverbs 18:24

AUTHOR / ARTIST

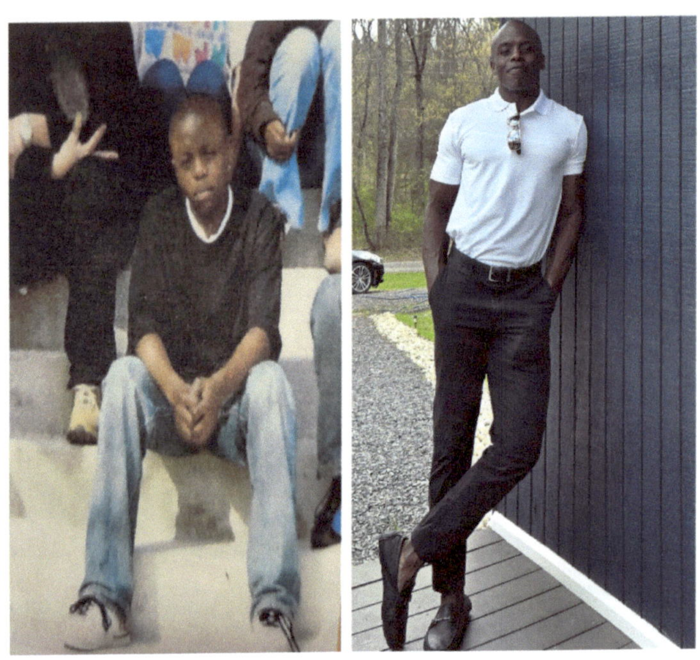

EDWARD ELLIOTT GABE

"THE ONLY WAY TO FLY, IS TO BELIEVE"

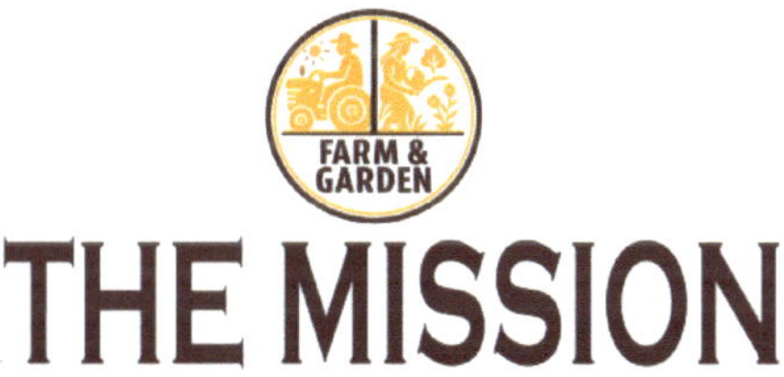

THE MISSION

Gifts and talents are only as valuable as what we do with them. Farm & Garden is a mission rooted in art, and nourished by the community. It is a way to cultivate hope by bringing people together through song and dance, praise and worship, sharing meals, and doing life side by side. The stories of the people are the heartbeat of my creativity—they inspire the art, shape the vision, and fuel the purpose.

An atmosphere where people can share joy, experience peace and be loved, practice patience, and grow in kindness. Where goodness is nurtured, faithfulness is celebrated, gentleness is welcomed, and discipline is strengthened.

Farm & Garden is a place where the fruits of the Spirit are not just spoken—they are lived. We create space for healing, restoration, and transformation. It's a farm and garden of grace, where every soul is invited to bloom.

The art and books are what support this mission as it continues to grow. Visit **ARTBE.ME** to learn more.

Author's Note

The contents of this book are intended to capture ideas and bring them to life through storytelling. While inspired by real people and experiences, the narratives presented are not direct representations of those individuals. Rather, they serve as creative interpretations—crafted to explore broader themes and evoke emotion. This work is a tribute to imagination, not documentation.

FREE FROM THE DARKNESS

30/30

Every April, millions around the world celebrate National Poetry Month—a time to honor the power of language, the beauty of expression, and the stories that live within us all. Poetry is more than words on a page; it is a mirror, a map, a melody. It helps us speak what's often left unsaid and listen to the quiet truths beneath the surface. In the spirit of this celebration, these next thirty pages are for you. Whether you are a seasoned writer or someone simply curious about your own voice, this space is yours to explore. Each page is an invitation to reflect, to imagine, to heal, to create. There are no right or wrong ways to write poetry. What matters is that you show up, pen in hand, and let your soul speak. So, during this month of poetry, take a moment each day to pause, breathe, and write. Let this be your garden of thought, where seeds of truth are planted, and every page is a chance to bloom.

1

2

3

4

5

6

7

8

9

10

11

12

13

15

16

17

18

19

21

25

27

ENCORE:

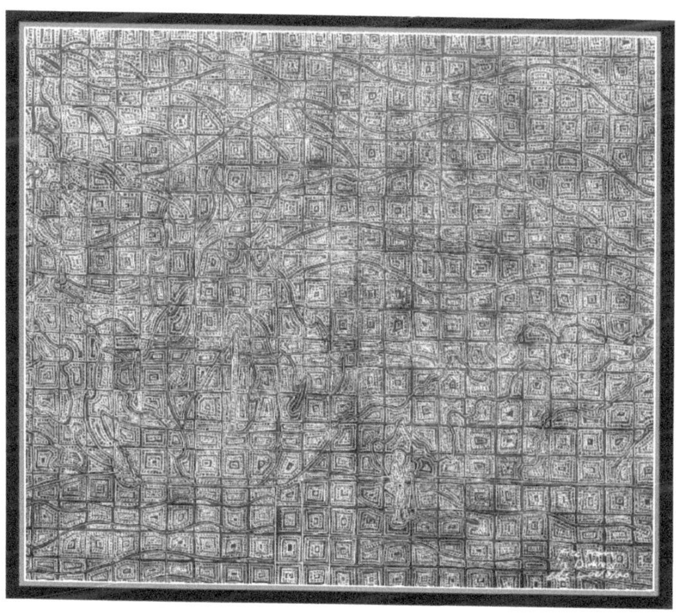

ART- "FREE FROM THE DARKNESS"

STILL, I GO ON

I am running, frantically chasing after my dreams.
Its cold outside and the snow is up to my knees.
The blistering cold air makes it hard to breathe,
But still, I go on.
There is no going back now,
For I have been running for far too long.
Visions of attaining my dreams in the pursuit,
Bring me hope, allowing me to go on.
Where my dream is running to, I do not know.
What I know is, where it goes, I will go.
The world will try to stop you,
And people, will slow you down.
The weight from the burdens of tomorrow,
Will distract you,
But through it all, you must prevail.
With the cold comes the hunger,
And we must kill to survive.
In hunger, you must be willing to fight,
For we fight to stay alive.
Therefore, I am running,
Frantically, chasing after my dreams.
In the cold, with the snow up to my knees.
The frozen elements make it hard to breathe,
But still, I go on.

www.ingramcontent.com/pod-product-compliance
Lightning Source LLC
LaVergne TN
LVHW052251100826
845147LV00001B/18

* 9 7 9 8 9 9 9 8 8 2 5 0 9 *